# PLYMOUTH

**IVYBRIDGE · KINGSAND · MII**
**NEWTON FERRERS · SALTASI**

**TOCK ·**

G000124156

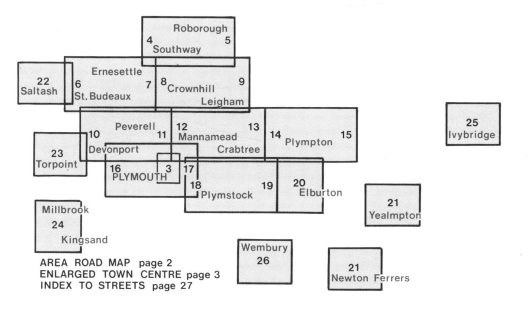

| | Roborough | |
| --- | --- | --- |
| 4 | Southway | 5 |

Ernesettle

| 22 Saltash | 6 St. Budeaux | 7 | 8 Crownhill | 9 |

Leigham

| 10 | Peverell | 11 | 12 Mannamead | 13 | 14 Plympton | 15 |

Devonport    Crabtree

| 23 Torpoint | 16 PLYMOUTH | 3 | 17 | | | 25 Ivybridge |

| | | 18 Plymstock | 19 | 20 Elburton |

| 24 Millbrook  Kingsand | | 21 Yealmpton |

**AREA ROAD MAP** page 2
**ENLARGED TOWN CENTRE** page 3
**INDEX TO STREETS** page 27

| Wembury 26 | 21 Newton Ferrers |

---

Every effort has been made to verify
the accuracy of information in this
book but the publishers cannot accept
responsibility for expense or loss
caused by an error or omission.
Information that will be of assistance
to the user of the maps will be welcomed.

The representation on these maps of a
road, track or path is no evidence of the
existence of a right of way.

| Car Park | P |
| --- | --- |
| Public Convenience | C |
| Place of Worship | + |
| One-way Street | → |
| Pedestrianized | ▨ |
| Post Office | ● |

**Scale of street plans 4 inches to 1 mile**
**Unless otherwise stated**

Street plans prepared and published by ESTATE PUBLICATIONS, Bridewell House, TENTERDEN, KENT.
The Publishers acknowledge the co-operation of the local authorities
of towns represented in this atlas.

**Ordnance Survey®** This product includes mapping data licensed from Ordnance Survey®
with the permission of the Controller of Her Majesty's Stationery Office.

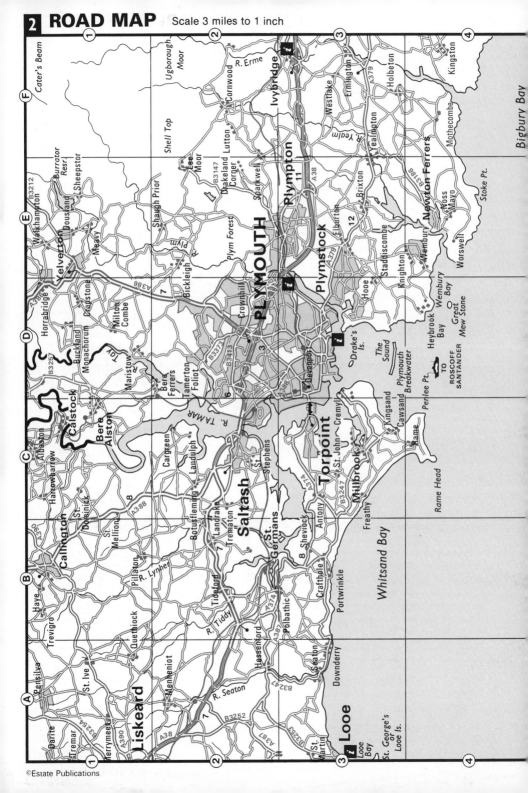

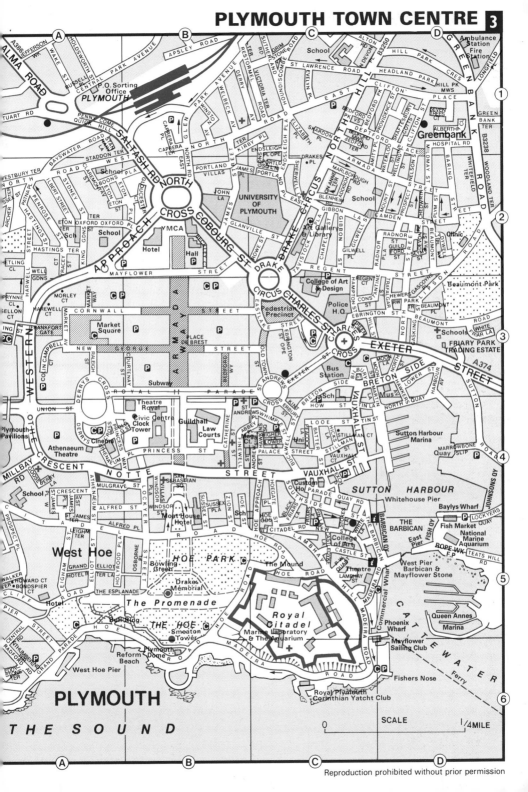

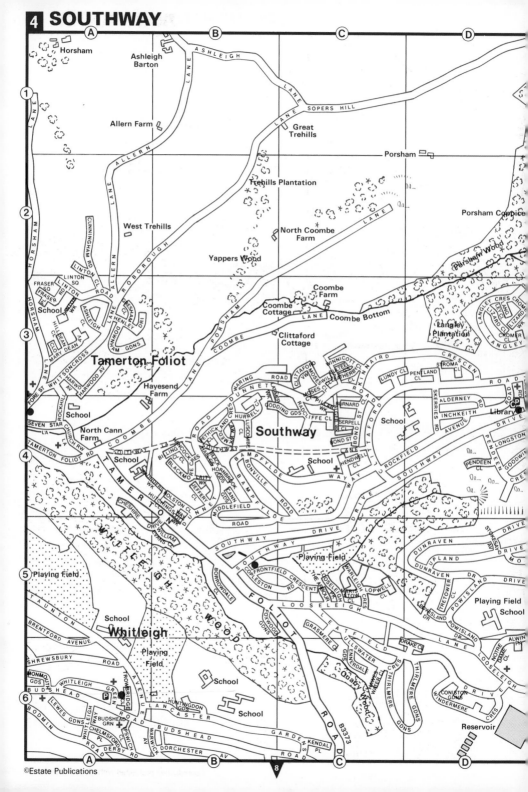

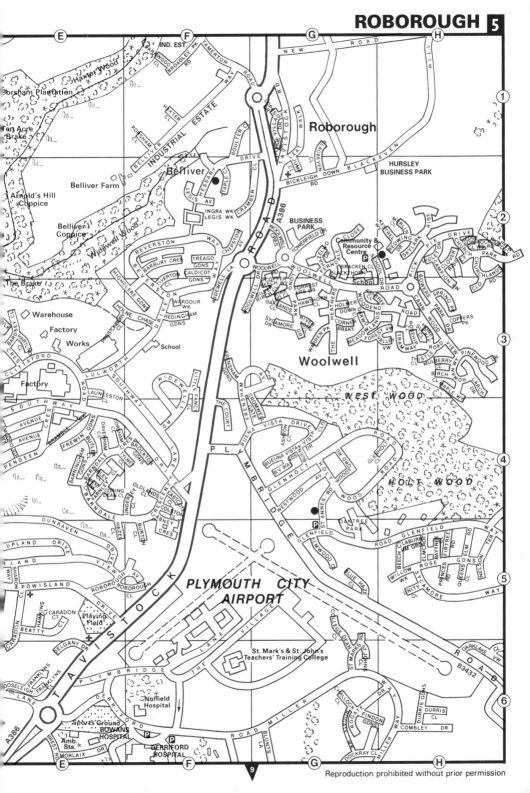

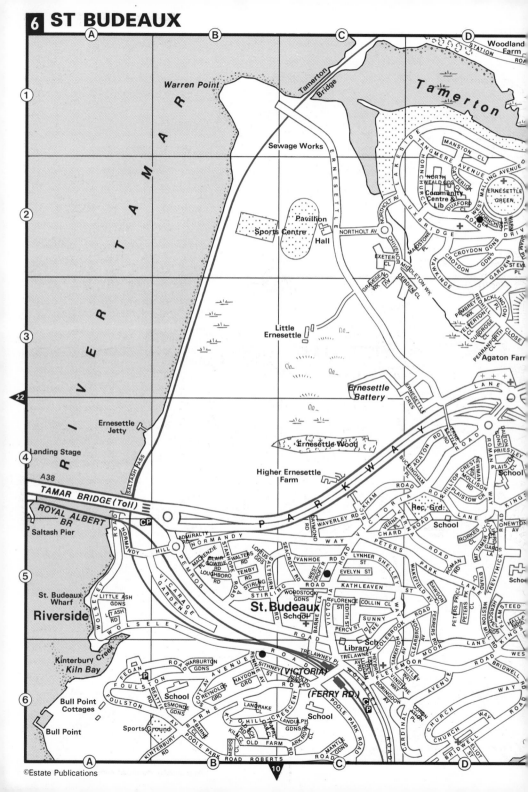

Woodland Farm
STATION ROAD

Tamerton

Warren Point

Tamerton Bridge

Sewage Works

MANSTON CL
LANGMERE AVENUE
CATERICK CL
HORNCHURCH
NORTH WEALD GDS
Community Centre & Lib
OXFORD CL
WEST MALLING AVENUE
ERNESETTLE GREEN
MARLBOROUGH DRIVE
MARHAM CL
HORNCHURCH
LAKESIDE

Pavillion
Hall
Sports Centre

NORTHOLT AV
NORTHOLT AV
CHURCH
MIDDLETON WK
MAIDSTONE PL
EXETER CL
GRAVESEND WK
DEBDEN CL
CROYDON GDNS
CROYDON
GARDENS
ST EVAL PL
HAWKINGE

PEMBREY WK
REDRUTH CL
YELVERTON WK
EVERTON CL
CULDROSE CL
PERRANPORTH CLOSE
ACKLINGTON
CLOSE

Little Ernesettle

Agaton Farm

Ernesettle Battery

ERNESETTLE
ERNESETTLE CRES
ERNESETTLE

LANE
ROMAN
BACON GDNS
PRIESTLEY
PLAISTER
School

Ernesettle Jetty

Ernesettle Wood

22

Landing Stage

AGATON ROAD
BUCKINGHAM ROAD
NEWMANS
CREST
HILLTOP
MOLLISON CR
PLAISTOW CR
NEWMAN RO
KINGS ROAD
RONEWTON
TREVITHICK

A38
TAMAR BRIDGE (Toll)
SALTASH PASS

Higher Ernesettle Farm

RICKHAM RO
WAVERLEY WAY
DAYMOND RD
VICTORIA ROAD
VERNA RD
CHARD
RORKES RD
PETERS PARK
ROMAN ROAD
MT TAMAR CL
TAGARS LA
WESTON MILL
BYARD

ROYAL ALBERT BR
Saltash Pier
CP

NORMANDY
NORMANDY HILL
ADMIRALTY
MACKENZIE PL
BLAIR RD
COWRIE RD
LOUGHBORO RD
WALTERS GDS
STANHOPE GDS
LOFTUS GDS
SALTBURN RD
TENBY RD
STIRLING RD
SEACROFT RD
IVANHOE RD
WEST CROFT
EVELYN ST
LYNHER ST
SHELLEY ST
WAKEFIELD RD
DAWSON RD
FERRERS RD
WESTON MILL LANE
CLEARBROOK
FLAMSTEED
HALL CL
School
Schoo

St. Budeaux Wharf
LITTLE ASH GDNS
LT ASH RD

Riverside
WOLSELEY ROAD
PEMROSE
VICARAGE GARDENS
WOLSELEY ROAD
STIRLING RD
WOODSTOCK GDNS
BARNE RD
KATHLEAVEN
COLLIN CL
EDITH RD
PERCY ST
SUNNY LANE
COLEBROOK AV
KITLEY
TAMERTON
HEYBROOK AV
STEED

St. Budeaux School

Kinterbury Creek
Kiln Bay

FEGAN ROAD
WARBURTON GDNS
BEATTIE RD
REYNOLDS RD
OTT AV AVENUE
HAYDON GRO
RENSITHNEY
ST BUDEAUX RD
VICTORIA
Library
Sch
TRELAWNEY PL
TRELAWNEY
FLETEMOOR
WOLSELEY ROAD
WINSTONE
BORINGDON
CORN GDNS
ELIOT ST
BRIDWELL
CHURCH WAY

Bull Point Cottages
FOULSTON
FOULSTON AV
ESMONDE GDNS
School
LANDRAKE CL
HILL CRESCENT
LANDULPH GDNS
OLD FARM
(FERRY RD)
CP
School
POOLE PARK ROAD
BRIDWELL ROAD
CHURCH WAY
BRIDWELL WAY

Bull Point
Sports Ground
KINTERBURY AV
BARNE
POOLE PARK ROAD
KILLIGREW
MIERS CL
POOLE PARK ROAD
ROBERTS ROAD
OLD FARM GDNS
PARK
MANTLE GDNS
ROAD

VICTORIA
(FERRY RD.)

10

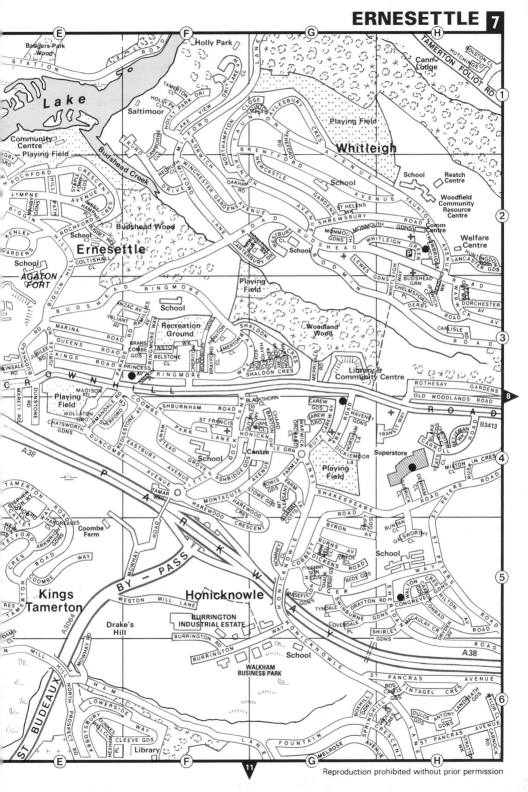

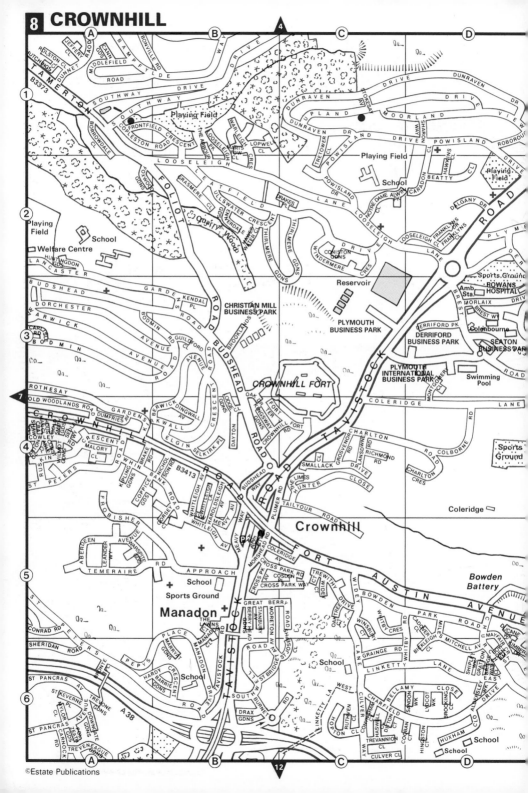

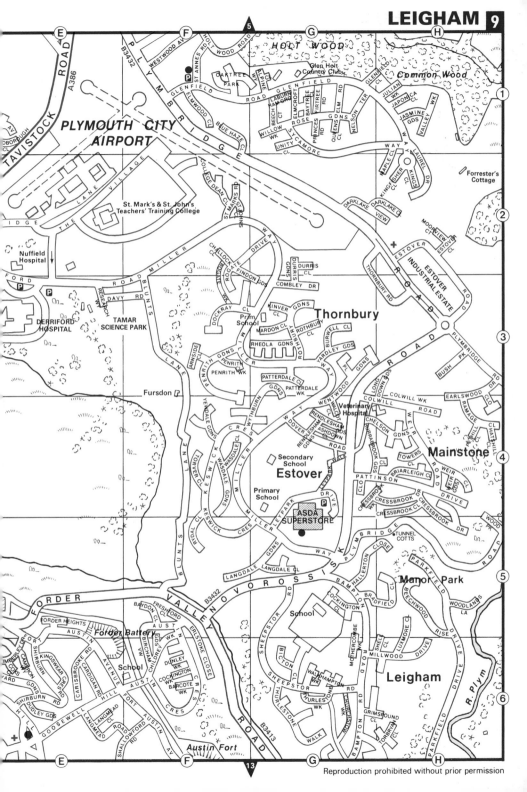

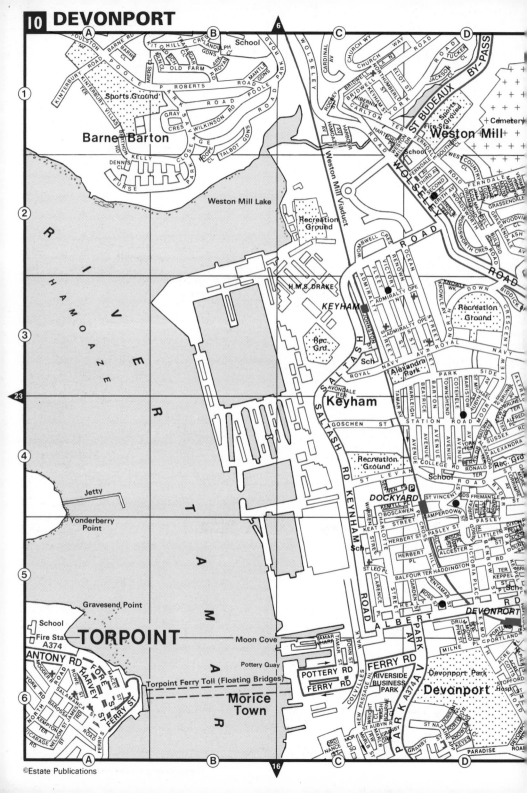

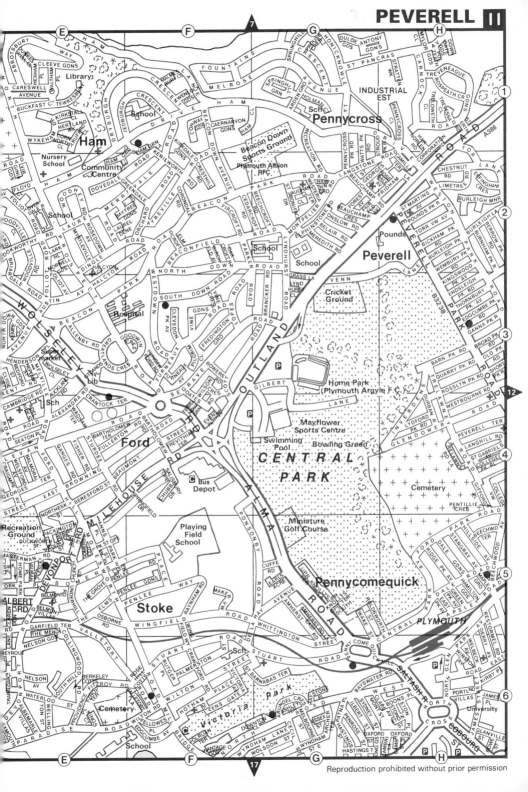

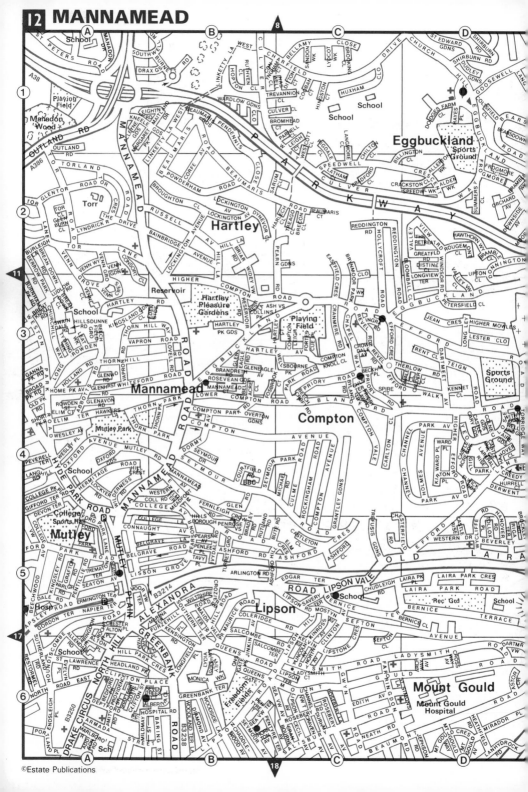

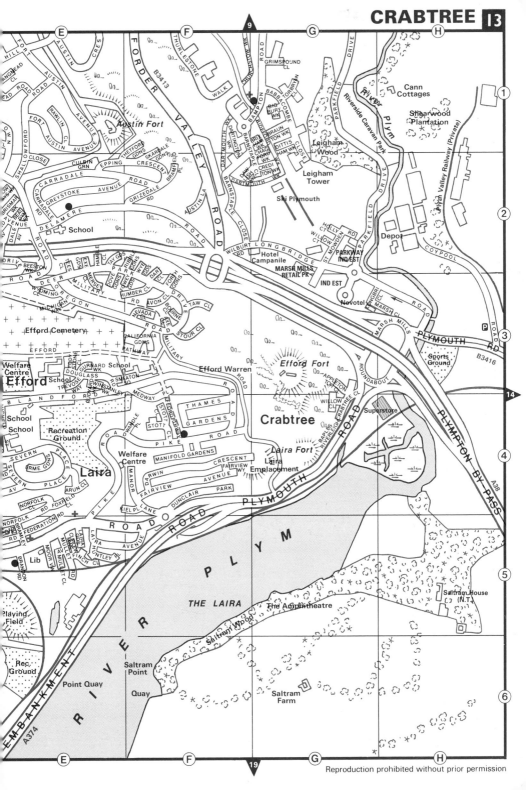

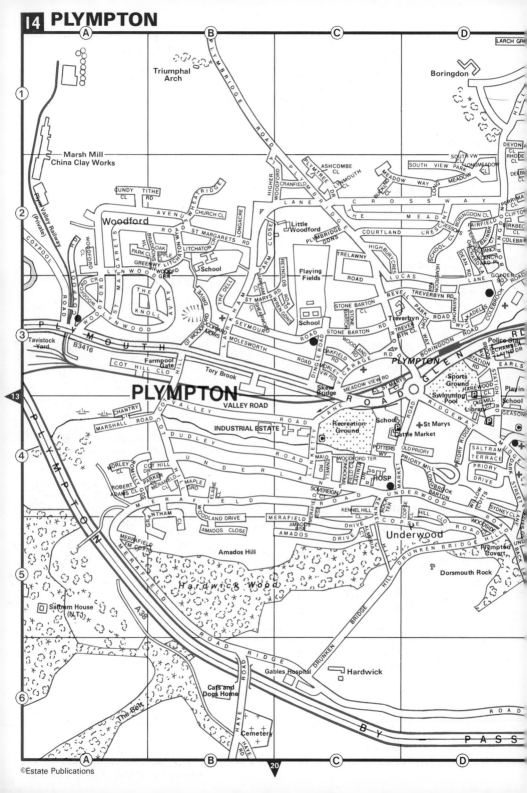

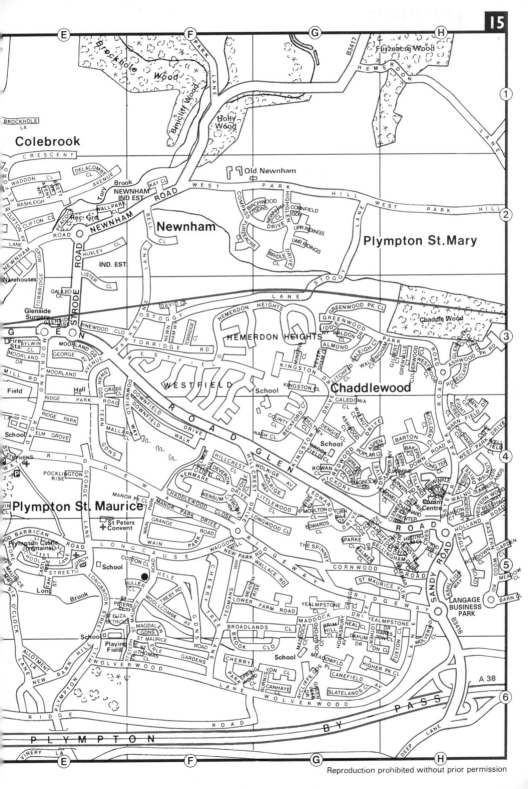

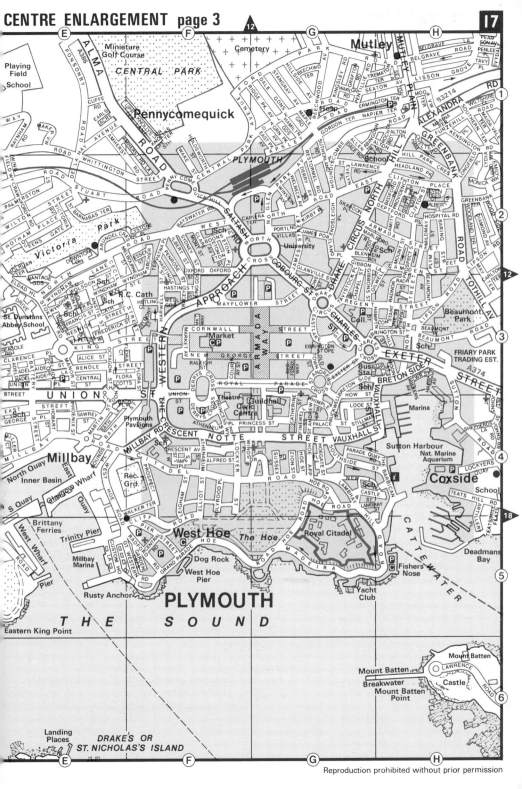

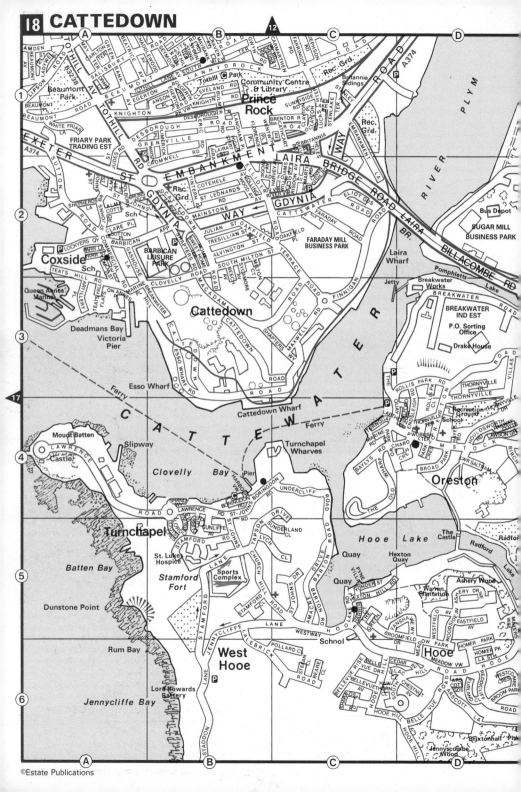

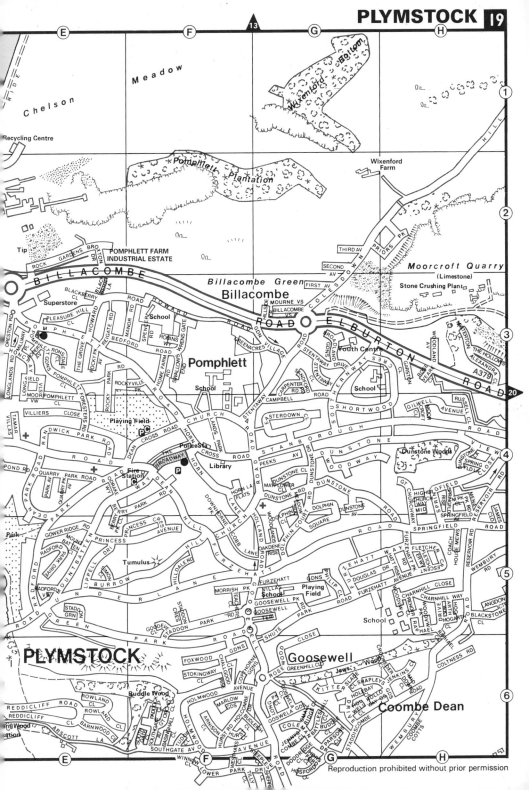

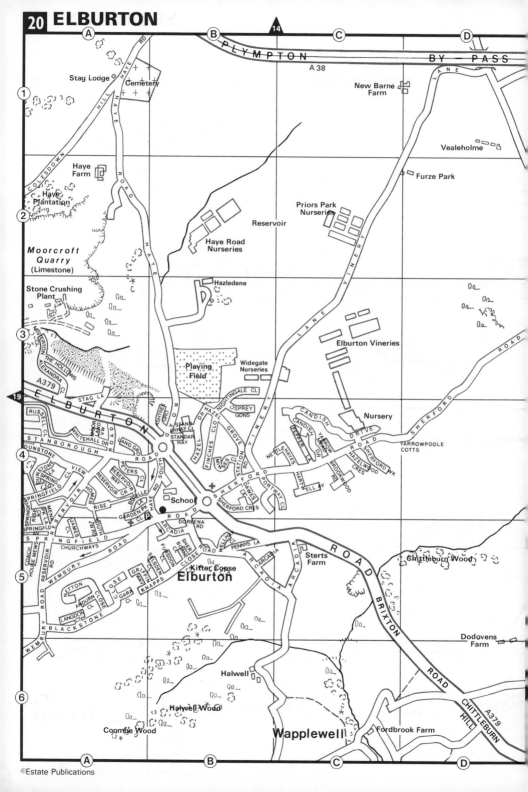

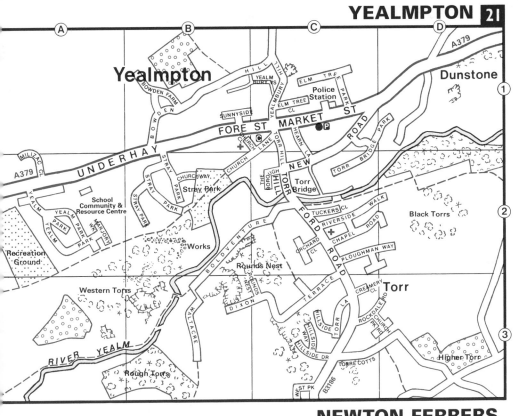

# NEWTON FERRERS

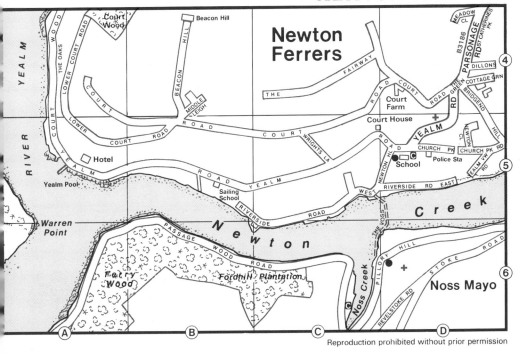

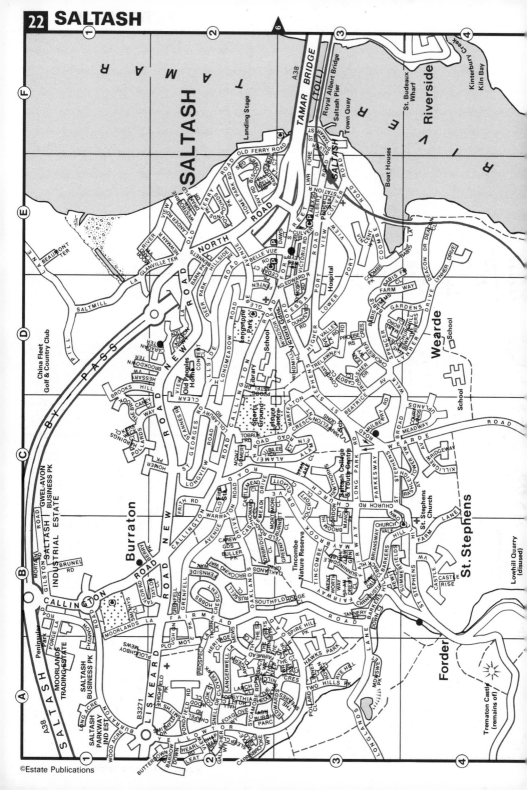

# 22 SALTASH

©Estate Publications

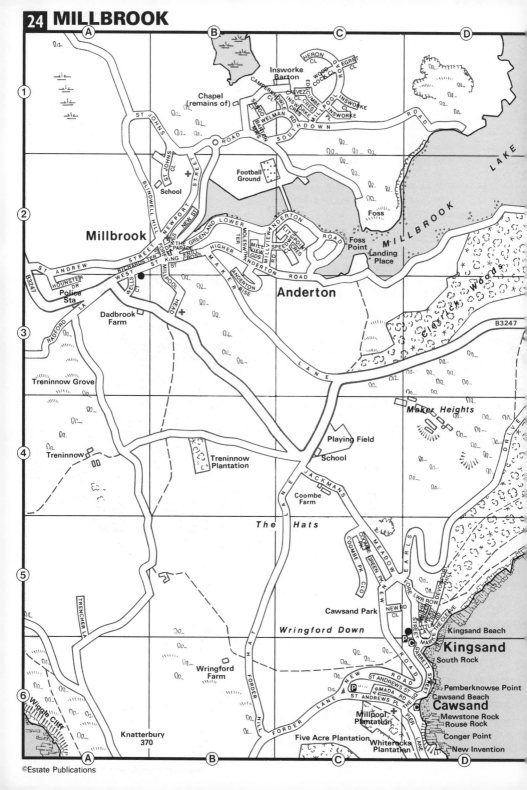

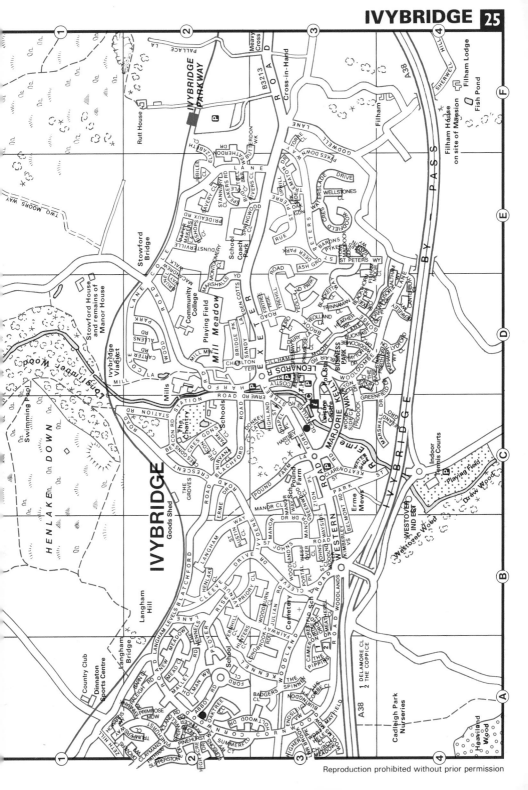

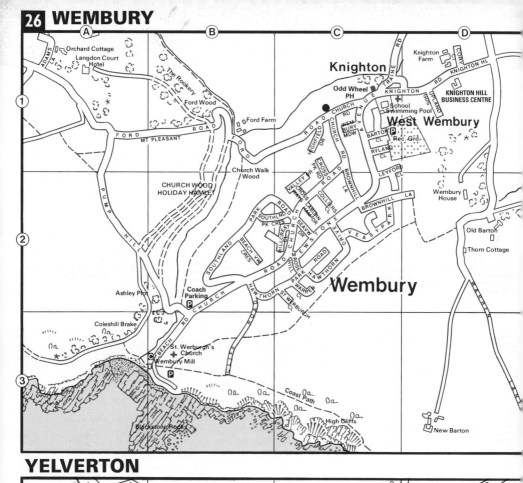

# YELVERTON

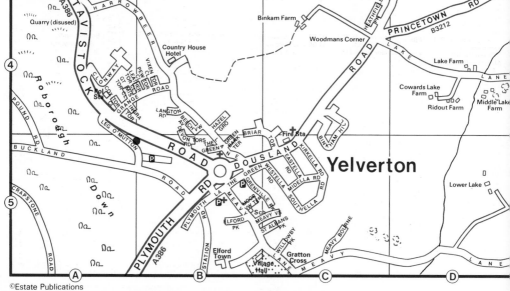

# A - Z  INDEX TO STREETS
## with Postcodes

The Index includes some names for which there is insufficient space on the maps. These names are preceded by an * and are followed by the nearest adjoining thoroughfare.

## PLYMOUTH

Dayton Clo. PL6 8 B4
De la Hay Av. PL3 17 E2
Dean Cross Rd. PL9 19 F4
Dean Hill. PL9 19 F4
Dean Park Rd. PL9 19 E4
Dean Rd. PL7 14 D2
Debden Clo. PL5 6 C2
Deeble Clo. PL7 14 D2
Deep La. PL9 15 H6
Deer Park Dri. PL3 13 E3
Defoe Clo. PL5 7 G5
Delacombe Clo. PL7 15 E2
Delamere Rd. PL6 13 E2
Delaware Gdns. PL2 10 D2
Delgany Dri. PL6 5 E6
*Delgany View, Delgany Dri. PL6 5 E6
*Delgany Villas, Delgany Dri. PL6 5 E6
Dengie Clo. PL7 15 G4
Denham Clo. PL5 7 H4
Dennis Clo. PL5 10 A2
Deptfort Pl. PL4 3 C1
Derby Rd. PL5 7 H3
Derriford Pk. PL6 8 D3
Derriford Rd. PL6 8 D2
Derry Av. PL4 3 B1
Derrys Cross. PL1 3 A3
Derwent Av. PL3 12 D4
Desborough La. PL4 18 B1
Desborough Rd. PL4 18 A1
Deveron Clo. PL7 15 F4
Devon Ter. PL3 12 A4
Devonia Clo. PL7 14 D1
Devonport Hill. PL1 16 C3
Devonport Rd. PL3 16 C2
*Devonshire Ho, Flora Cotts. PL1 17 E3
Devonshire St. PL4 3 D2
Diamond Av. PL4 17 H2
Dickens Rd. PL5 7 G5
Dickiemoor La. PL5 7 G4
Dieppe Clo. PL1 16 C3
Digby Gro. PL5 7 E1
Dingle Rd, Ham. PL2 11 E2
Dingle Rd, Plympton. PL7 14 C3
Dingwall Av. PL5 8 B4
Distine Clo. PL3 12 D2
Dittisham Walk. PL6 13 G1
Ditton Ct. PL6 12 C1
Dixon Pl. PL2 16 C1
Dockray Clo. PL6 9 F3
Doddridge Clo. PL9 19 G6
Doidges Farm Clo. PL6 12 D1
Dolphin Clo. PL9 19 G5
Dolphin Court Rd. PL9 19 G5
Dolphin Sq. PL9 19 G4
Donnington Dri. PL3 12 D2
Dorchester Av. PL5 8 A3
Doreena Rd. PL9 20 B5
Dormy Av. PL3 12 B4
Douglas Dri. PL9 19 G5
Douglass Rd. PL3 13 E3
Dove Gdns. PL3 13 E3
Dovedale Rd. PL2 11 E2
Dover Rd. PL6 9 G4
Down Rd. PL7 15 H4
Downfield Dri. PL7 15 F4
Downfield Walk. PL7 15 F3
Downfield Way. PL7 15 F4
Downgate Gdns. PL2 11 H1
Downham Gdns. PL5 4 A3
Downhorne Pk. PL9 19 F5
Downside Av. PL6 12 D2
Downton Clo. PL1 11 F6
Drake Circus. PL4 3 C2
Drake Clo. PL6 4 C6
Drake Ct. PL4 18 A1
Drake Way. PL9 19 E4
*Drakes Island Ho, Custom Ho La. PL1 17 E5
Drakes Pl. PL4 3 C2
Drax Gdns. PL6 12 B1
Drayton Rd. PL5 7 G6
Drummond Clo. PL2 10 D2
Drummond Pl. PL1 16 C2
Drunken Bridge Hill. PL7 14 C6
Dryburgh Cres. PL2 11 E1
Dryden Av. PL5 7 H5
Ducane Walk. PL6 8 D5
Duckworth St. PL2 16 C1
Dudley Gdns. PL6 12 D1
Dudley Rd. PL7 14 B4
*Duke Rock, Custom Ho La. PL1 17 E5
Duke St. PL1 16 B3
Duloe Gdns. PL2 11 G1
Dumfries Av. PL5 8 A4
Duncan St. PL1 16 B3
Dunclair Park. PL3 13 F4
Duncombe Av. PL5 7 E4
Dundas St. PL2 16 D1
Dundonald St. PL2 16 C1
Dunkeswell Clo. PL2 11 E1
Dunley Walk. PL6 9 F6
Dunnet Rd. PL6 8 A1
Dunraven Dri. PL6 8 C1
Dunster Clo. PL7 15 H5
Dunstone Av. PL9 19 G4
Dunstone Clo. PL9 19 G4
Dunstone Dri. PL9 19 G4
Dunstone La. PL9 19 H4
Dunstone Rd, Higher St Budeaux. PL5 7 E4
Dunstone Rd, Plymstock. PL9 19 G4
Dunstone View. PL9 19 G4
Durban Rd. PL3 11 H4
Durham Av. PL4 12 C6
*Durham Cotts, Cecil St. PL1 17 E2
Durnford St. PL1 16 D4
Durnford St Ope. PL1 16 D4
Durrant Clo. PL1 16 B2
Durris Clo. PL6 9 G2
Durris Gdns. PL6 9 G2
Durwent Clo. PL9 18 B5
Duxford Clo. PL5 6 D2
Dynevor Clo. PL3 12 B2

Eagle Rd. PL7 15 H5
Earls Acre. PL3 17 E1
Earls Mill Rd. PL7 14 D3
Earlswood Clo. PL6 9 H4
Earlswood Dri. PL6 9 H3
East Park Av. PL4 17 G1
East St. PL1 17 E4
*East Vw, Ann's Pl. PL3 16 C1
Eastbury Av. PL5 7 F4
Eastcote Clo. PL6 5 F4
Easterdown Clo. PL9 19 G4
Eastern Wood Rd. PL7 15 H5
Eastfield Av. PL9 18 D5
Eastfield Cres. PL3 12 C3
Eastlake St. PL1 3 C3
Ebrington St. PL4 3 C3
Ebrington St Ope. PL4 3 C3
*Eddy Thomas Walk, Whitleigh Grn. PL5 7 H2
Eddystone Clo. PL9 13 E3
Eddystone Ter. PL1 3 A6
Edenside. PL3 12 B3
Edgar Ter. PL4 12 C5
Edgcumbe Av. PL1 16 D2
*Edgcumbe Ho, Union St. PL1 3 A4
Edgcumbe Pk Rd. PL3 11 H3
Edgcumbe St. PL1 16 D4
Edinburgh St. PL1 16 B4
Edith Av. PL4 12 C6
Edith St. PL5 6 C5
Edna Ter. PL4 18 B1
Edwards Clo. PL7 15 G5
Edwards Dri. PL7 15 G4
Effingham Cres. PL3 11 H2
Efford Cres. PL3 12 C3
Efford La. PL3 12 D5
Efford Pathway. PL3 13 E3
Efford Rd. PL3 12 D3
Efford Walk. PL3 12 C3
Egerton Cres. PL4 18 B1
Egerton Pl. PL4 18 B1
Egerton Rd. PL4 18 A1
Eggbuckland Rd. PL3 12 D1
Eight Acres Clo. PL7 15 H4
Elaine Clo. PL7 14 B4
Elburton Rd. PL9 19 G3
Eldad Hill. PL1 17 E3
Elder Clo. PL7 15 G4
Elford Cres. PL7 15 E2
Elford Dri. PL9 18 D4
Elgin Cres. PL5 8 B4
Elim Ct. PL3 12 A4
Elim Ter. PL3 12 A4
Eliot Gdns. PL4 18 C2
Eliot St. PL5 10 C1
Elizabeth Pl. PL4 3 C1
Elliot Rd. PL4 18 B2
Elliot St. PL1 3 A5
Elliot Ter La. PL1 3 A5
*Elm Cotts, Fore St. PL7 15 E5
Elm Cres. PL3 12 C5
Elm Croft. PL6 5 H5
Elm Gro. PL7 15 E4
Elm Rd, Glenholt Park. PL6 9 G1
Elm Rd, Mannamead. PL4 12 B4
Elm Ter. PL4 12 B4
Elmcroft. PL2 11 F2
Elmwood Clo. PL6 5 G5
Elphinstone Rd. PL2 11 G2
Elwick Gdns. PL3 12 D4
Embankment La. PL4 18 C1
Embankment Rd. PL4 18 B2
*Embankment Rd La Nth, Cathcart Av. PL4 18 C1
Emily Gdns. PL4 12 B6
Emma Pl. PL1 16 D4
Emma Pl Ope. PL1 16 D4
Endsleigh Gdns. PL4 3 C2
Endsleigh Park Rd. PL3 11 H3
Endsleigh Pl. PL4 3 C2
Endsleigh Pl Ope. PL4 3 C1
Endsleigh Rd. PL9 18 D4
Ennerdale Gdns. PL6 8 B2
Epping Cres. PL6 13 E2
Epworth Ter. PL2 10 D4
Eric Rd. PL4 18 B1
Erith Av. PL2 10 D2
Erle Gdns. PL7 15 F6
Erlstoke Clo. PL6 9 F5
Erme Gdns. PL3 13 E4
Ermington Ter. PL4 17 G1
Ernesettle Cres. PL5 6 D3
Ernesettle Grn. PL5 6 D1
Ernesettle La. PL5 6 C2
Ernesettle Rd. PL5 6 D4
Esmonde Gdns. PL5 6 B6
Essex St. PL1 3 A2
Esso Wharf Rd. PL4 18 B3
Estover Clo. PL6 9 H2
Estover Rd. PL6 9 H2
Eton Av. PL1 3 A2
Eton Pl. PL1 3 A2
Eton St. PL1 3 A2
Eton Ter. PL1 3 A2
Evans Pl. PL2 11 F4
Evelyn Pl. PL4 3 C1
Evelyn St. PL5 6 C5
Exchange St. PL1 3 C4
Exe Gdns. PL3 13 E2
Exeter Clo. PL5 6 C2
Exeter St. PL4 3 C3
Exmouth Rd. PL1 16 C2

Fairfax Ter. PL2 10 D4
Fairfield. PL7 14 D2
Fairfield Av. PL2 11 G2
Fairview Av. PL3 13 F4
Fairview Way. PL3 13 F4
Fanshawe Way. PL9 18 C5
Faraday Rd. PL4 18 C2
*Fareham Cotts, Cattledown Rd. PL4 18 B2
Farm Clo. PL7 14 B2
Farm La, Eggbuckland. PL6 12 D1
Farm La, Honicknowle. PL5 7 G4
Farnley Clo. PL6 5 E4
Farringdon Rd. PL4 18 C1
Federation Rd. PL3 13 E5
Fegan Rd. PL5 6 A6
Fellowes La. PL1 16 D2
Fellowes Pl. PL1 16 D2
Fern Clo. PL7 15 H4
Ferndale Av. PL2 10 D2
Ferndale Clo. PL6 5 G2
Ferndale Rd. PL2 10 D1
Fernleigh Rd. PL3 12 B4
Ferrers Rd. PL5 6 D5
Ferry Rd. PL1 16 B2
Ferry St. PL11 10 A6
Feversham Clo. PL7 15 G3
Finch Clo. PL3 13 E5
Finches Clo. PL9 20 B4
Findon Gdns. PL6 5 G6
Finewell St. PL1 3 B4
Finnigan Rd. PL4 18 C3
Fircroft Rd. PL2 11 F2
First Av, Billacombe. PL9 19 G3
First Av, Stoke. PL1 16 D3
Firtree Rd. PL6 9 G1
Fisher Rd. PL2 11 E4
Fitzroy Rd. PL1 16 D2
Fitzroy Ter. PL1 11 E6
Flamborough Rd. PL6 4 D3
Flamborough Way. PL6 5 E4
Flamsteed Cres. PL5 6 D5
Fleet St. PL2 10 C3
Fletcher Cres. PL9 19 H5
Fletcher Way. PL9 19 H5
Fletemoor Rd. PL5 6 C6
Flora Cotts. PL1 17 E3
Flora Ct. PL1 17 E3
Flora St. PL1 17 F3
Florence Pl. PL4 18 B1
Florence St. PL5 6 C5
Floyd Clo. PL2 11 E2
Foliot Av. PL2 11 E3
Foliot Rd. PL2 11 E2
Ford Hill. PL2 11 E4
Ford Park. PL4 12 A5
Ford Park La. PL4 12 A5
Ford Park Rd. PL4 17 F1
Forder Heights. PL6 9 E5
Forder Valley Rd. PL6 13 F1
Fore St, Devonport. PL1 16 B3
Fore St, Plympton. PL7 15 E5
Fore St, Tamerton Foliot. PL5 4 A4
Forest Av. PL2 11 G2
Forest View. PL6 5 G3
Foresters Rd. PL9 19 E4
Forge Clo. PL6 5 G1
Forresters Dri. PL9 5 G3
Forster Clo. PL7 15 H5
Fort Austin Av. PL6 8 C5
Fort Ter. PL6 8 B4
Fortescue Pl. PL3 12 C3
Forth Gdns. PL3 13 F3
Fosbrook Ct. PL3 12 B4
Foulston Av. PL5 10 A1
Fountains Cres. PL2 11 F1
Fowey Gdns. PL3 13 F3
Foxfield Clo. PL3 13 E4
Foxtor Clo. PL5 7 G3
Foxwood Gdns, Plymstock. PL9 19 F6
Foxwood Gdns, Whitleigh. PL6 8 A2
Foyle Clo. PL7 15 F4
Francis Pl. PL1 17 E3
Francis St. PL1 17 E3
Frankfort Gate. PL1 3 A3
Franklyns. PL6 5 E6
Franklyns Clo. PL6 8 D2
Fraser Pl. PL5 4 A3
Fraser Rd. PL5 4 A3
Fraser Sq. PL5 4 A3
Frederick St East. PL1 17 E3
Frederick St West. PL1 17 E3
Fredington Gro. PL2 11 F3
*Freedom Sq, Lydia Way. PL4 12 B6
Freemantle Gdns. PL2 10 D4
Fremantle Pl. PL2 10 D4
Frensham Av. PL6 5 F4
Frensham Gdns. PL6 5 F3
Freshford Clo. PL6 9 F5
*Freshford Walk Freshford Clo. PL6 9 F5
Frewin Gdns. PL6 5 E4
Friars La. PL1 3 C4
Frobisher App. PL 8 A4
Frogmore Av. PL6 12 D2
Frogmore Ct. PL6 12 D2
Frome Clo. PL7 15 F4
Frontfield Cres. PL6 8 A1
Fullerton Rd. PL2 11 E4
Furland Clo. PL9 18 D6
Furneaux Av. PL2 11 F3
Furneaux Rd. PL2 11 F3
Fursdon Clo. PL9 20 B5
Furze Park. PL5 10 A2
Furzeacre Clo. PL7 15 G2
Furzehatt Av. PL9 19 G5
Furzehatt Park Rd. PL9 19 H5
Furzehatt Rise. PL9 19 H5
Furzehatt Rd. PL9 19 F5
Furzehatt Villas. PL9 19 G5
Furzehatt Way. PL9 19 G5
Furzehill Rd. PL4 17 H1

Galileo Clo. PL7 15 E3
Galsworthy Clo. PL5 7 H5
Ganges Rd. PL2 11 E4
Ganna Park Rd. PL3 11 H3
Gara Clo. PL9 20 A5
Garden Clo. PL7 15 H5
Garden Cres. PL1 17 F5
Garden Park Clo. PL9 20 A4
Garden St. PL2 16 B1
Garden Village. PL9 19 G3
Gards La. PL5 6 D5
Garfield Ter. PL1 11 E5
Garrick Clo. PL5 7 H4
Garrison Clo. PL1 16 B4
Garston Clo. PL9 19 H3
Gascoyne Pl. PL4 3 D3
Gashouse La. PL4 18 A2
Gasking St. PL4 3 D3
Gdynia Way. PL4 18 B2
Geasons La. PL7 14 D4
George Av. PL7 15 E3
George La. PL7 15 E4
George Pl. PL1 17 E4
George Sq. PL1 16 C3
George St. PL1 16 C3
Gibbon La. PL4 3 C2
Gibbon St. PL4 3 C2
Gifford Pl. PL3 11 H4
Gifford Ter Rd. PL3 12 A4
Gilbert Ct. PL7 15 H3
Gilbert La. PL2 11 G3
Gill Pk. PL3 12 D4
Gilwell Av. PL9 19 H4
Gilwell Pl. PL4 3 C2
Gilwell St. PL4 3 C2
Glanville St. PL4 3 B2
Glen Park Av. PL4 3 B1
Glen Rd, Mannamead. PL3 12 B4
Glen Rd, Plympton. PL7 14 D3
Glenavon Rd. PL3 12 A4
Glenburn Clo. PL3 12 A2
Glendower Rd. PL3 11 H4
Gleneagle Av. PL3 12 B3
Gleneagle Rd. PL3 12 B3
Glenfield Clo. PL6 9 G1
Glenfield Rd. PL6 9 F1
Glenfield Way. PL6 9 G1
Glenhaven Clo. PL7 15 H3
Glenholt Clo. PL6 5 H4
Glenholt Rd. PL6 5 G4
Glenhurst Rd. PL3 12 A3
Glenmore Av. PL2 10 D4
Glenside Rise. PL7 15 E3
Glentor Rd. PL3 12 A2
Glenwood Rd. PL3 12 A3
Gloucester Ct. PL1 3 B2
Goad Av. PL4 18 B2
Godding Gdns. PL6 4 C4
*Godolphin Ter, Molesworth Rd. PL3 16 D1
Golden Sq. PL7 14 D3
Goldsmith Gdns. PL5 8 A4
Goodeve Clo. PL9 19 F5
Goodwin Av. PL6 4 D4
Goodwin Cres. PL2 11 F3
Gooseberry La. PL1 3 A4
Goosewell Hill. PL6 12 D1
Goosewell Pk Rd. PL9 19 G5
Goosewell Rd. PL9 19 G5
Goosewell Ter. PL9 19 G5
Gordon Ter. PL4 17 G1
Gorsey Clo. PL5 8 B4
Goschen St. PL1 10 C4
Goswela Clo. PL9 19 G6
Goswela Gdns. PL9 19 G6
Gower Ridge Rd. PL9 19 E5
Grafton Rd. PL4 17 G1
Grainge Rd. PL6 8 C6
Granby Ct. PL1 16 B3
Granby Grn. PL1 16 B2
Granby Pl. PL1 16 B3
Granby St. PL1 16 B2
Granby Way. PL1 16 B3
Grand Hotel Rd. PL1 3 A5
Grand Par. PL1 3 A6
*Grange Cotts, George La. PL7 15 E4
Grange Rd. PL7 15 F5
Grantham Clo. PL7 14 B4
Grantley Gdns. PL3 12 C5
Grasmere Clo. PL6 8 B2
Grass La. PL2 11 G3
Grassendale Av. PL2 10 D2
Gratton Pl. PL6 8 D6
Gravesend Walk. PL5 6 C3
Gray Cres. PL5 10 B1

32

Rowan Way. PL6 5 H3
Rowden St. PL3 12 A4
Rowdown Clo. PL7 15 H5
Rowe St. PL4 3 C2
Rowland Clo. PL9 19 E6
Royal Navy Av. PL2 10 C3
Royal Par. PL1 3 B3
Royal William Rd. PL1 16 D5
Rudyard Walk. PL3 13 E3
Rufford Clo. PL2 11 E1
Ruskin Cres. PL4 8 A4
Russell Av. PL3 12 B2
Russell Clo. PL9 19 H4
Russell Pl. PL4 3 A1
Russet Wood. PL5 7 E3
Rutger Pl. PL1 16 D2
Ruthven Clo. PL6 12 B1
Rutland Rd. PL4 12 B5
Rydal Clo. PL6 9 F5
Ryder Rd. PL6 16 C1

St Andrew St. PL1 3 C4
St Andrews Cross. PL1 3 C3
St Andrews Pl. PL1 3 C4
St Annes Rd. PL6 9 F1
St Aubyn Av. PL2 10 D4
St Aubyn Rd. PL1 16 B2
St Aubyn St. PL1 16 B2
St Barnabas Ter. PL1 17 E2
St Boniface Clo. PL2 11 G2
St Boniface Dri. PL2 11 G2
St Bridget Av. PL6 8 B6
St Budeaux By-Pass. PL5 7 E6
St Dunstans Ter. PL4 18 B1
St Edward Gdns. PL6 12 D1
St Elizabeth Clo. PL7 15 E5
St Erth Rd. PL2 11 H1
St Eval Pl. PL5 6 D2
St Francis Ct. PL5 7 F4
St Gabriels Av. PL3 11 H4
St Georges Av. PL2 11 G2
St Georges Ter. PL2 10 D4
St Helens Walk. PL5 7 G2
St Hilary Ter. PL4 18 B1
St James Pl East. PL1 3 A4
St James Pl West. PL1 3 A4
St James Rd. PL11 10 A6
St James Ter. PL1 3 A4
St Johns Bridge Rd. PL4 17 H4
St Johns Clo. PL6 5 G6
St Johns Dri. PL9 18 C5
St Johns Rd, Cattedown. PL4 18 A2
St Johns Rd, Turnchapel. PL9 18 B4
St Johns St. PL4 17 H4
St Josephs Clo. PL6 8 C6
St Judes Rd. PL4 18 A2
St Keverne Pl. PL2 8 A6
*St Lawrence Mews, St Lawrence Rd. PL4 3 C1
St Lawrence Rd. PL4 3 C1
St Leo Pl. PL2 16 B1
St Leonards Rd. PL4 18 B2
St Levan Rd. PL2 10 C4
St Margarets Rd. PL7 14 A3
St Marks Rd. PL6 5 G6
St Martins Av. PL3 11 H2
St Mary St. PL1 16 D3
St Marys Ct. PL7 14 C3
St Marys Ct. PL7 14 C3
St Marys Ter. PL7 14 B3
St Maurice Mews. PL7 15 F5
St Maurice Rd. PL7 15 F5
St Maurice Vw. PL7 15 H5
*St Mawes Ter, Berkshire Dri. PL2 10 D4
St Michael Av. PL3 10 D3
St Michaels Clo. PL1 16 B4
St Michaels Ter. PL1 16 C2
St Mowden Rd. PL2 13 G2
St Nazaire App. PL1 16 B2
St Nazaire Rd. PL1 16 B2
St Pancras Av. PL2 11 G1
St Paul St. PL1 16 D5
St Pauls Clo. PL3 13 E4
St Peters Clo. PL7 15 E5
St Peters Ct. PL1 17 E3
St Peters Rd. PL5 8 A4
St Simons La. PL4 12 D6
St Stephens Pl. PL7 15 F6
St Stephens Rd. PL7 15 F6
St Stephens St. PL1 16 B4

*St Thereses Ct, Fore St. PL1 16 B3
St Thomas Clo. PL7 15 F6
St Vincent St. PL2 10 D4
Salamanca St. PL11 10 A6
Salcombe Rd. PL4 12 B5
Salcombe Ter. PL4 12 B6
Salisbury Ope. PL4 11 F4
Salisbury Rd. PL4 18 A1
Saltash Pass. PL5 6 A4
Saltash Rd, Keyham. PL2 10 C3
Saltash Rd, Plymouth. PL3 3 B1
Saltburn Rd. PL5 6 B5
Saltram Ter. PL7 14 D4
San Sebastian Sq. PL1 3 B4
Sandford Rd. PL9 19 G3
Sandon Walk. PL6 12 C1
Sandy Rd. PL7 15 H5
Sarum Clo. PL3 12 B2
Saunders Walk. PL6 4 A4
Savage Rd. PL5 10 B1
Savery Ter. PL4 12 C5
Sawrey St. PL1 17 E4
School Clo. PL7 14 D2
School Dri. PL6 5 H2
School La. PL7 15 E5
Scott Av. PL5 6 B6
Scott Rd. PL2 11 F3
Sea View Av. PL4 12 C6
Sea View Ter. PL4 12 B6
*Sea View Villas, St Georges Av. PL2 11 G2
Seacroft Rd. PL5 6 C5
Seaton Av. PL4 17 H1
Seaton La. PL4 17 H1
Seaton Pl. PL2 11 E4
Second Av, Billacombe. PL9 19 G2
Second Av, Stoke. PL1 16 D3
Second Av, Weston Mill. PL2 10 D2
Sedley Way. PL5 8 A4
Sefton Av. PL4 12 C5
Sefton Clo. PL4 12 C6
Segrave Rd. PL2 11 F3
Selkirk Pl. PL5 8 B4
Sellon Ct. PL1 3 A3
Selsden Clo. PL9 20 B5
Sennen Pl. PL2 10 C4
Serpell Clo. PL6 4 C4
Seven Stars La. PL6 4 C4
Seven Trees Ct. PL4 3 D1
Severn Pl. PL3 13 E4
*Sewell Ct, Langhill Rd. PL3 11 H4
Seymour Av. PL4 18 B1
Seymour Dri. PL3 12 B4
*Seymour Mews, Thornton Av. PL4 12 B6
Seymour Park. PL3 3 B4
Seymour Rd, Mannamead. PL3 12 B4
Seymour Rd, Plympton. PL7 14 B3
Seymour St. PL4 3 D2
Shaftesbury Cotts. PL4 3 D1
*Shaftesbury Ct, Shaftesbury Cotts. PL4 3 D1
Shakespeare Rd. PL5 7 G4
Shaldon Cres. PL5 7 G3
Shallowford Clo. PL6 13 E2
Shallowford Rd. PL6 13 E2
Shapleys Gdns. PL9 19 G6
Shapters Rd. PL4 18 B2
Shapters Way. PL4 18 C3
Sharon Way. PL6 8 D1
Sharrose Rd. PL9 19 H6
Shaw Way. PL9 18 B4
Shearwood Clo. PL7 14 B3
Sheepstor Rd. PL6 9 G6
Shell Clo. PL6 9 H6
Shelley Way. PL5 6 C5
Shepherds La. PL4 17 H4
Sherborne Clo. PL9 20 B5
Sherford Cres, Higher St Budeaux. PL5 7 E4
Sherford Cres, Elburton. PL9 20 B4
Sherford Rd. PL9 20 B4
Sherford Walk. PL9 20 C4
Sheridan Rd. PL3 8 A6
Sherril Clo. PL9 19 G6
Sherwell La. PL4 3 C2

Shipley Walk. PL6 8 D6
Shirburn Rd. PL6 12 D1
Shirley Gdns. PL5 7 H5
Short Park Rd. PL3 11 H3
Shortwood Cres. PL9 19 G4
Shrewsbury Rd. PL5 7 G2
Shute Park Rd. PL9 19 G5
*Sidmouth Cotts, Westhill Rd. PL4 12 B5
Silver Birch Clo. PL6 5 G3
Simon Clo. PL9 19 E5
Sir John Hawkins Sq. PL1 3 C4
Sithney St. PL5 6 B6
Six O'Clock La. PL7 15 E5
Skardale Gdns. PL6 13 F1
Skardon Pl. PL4 3 C1
Skerries Rd. PL6 4 D4
Skylark Rise. PL6 5 H2
Slade Clo. PL9 19 G6
Slatelands Clo. PL7 15 G6
Smallack Clo. PL6 8 C4
Smallack Dri. PL6 8 C4
Smallridge Clo. PL9 19 H6
Smeaton Sq. PL3 13 E3
Somerset Cotts. PL3 16 D1
Somerset Pl. PL3 16 D1
Sopers Hill. PL5 4 C1
South Down Rd. PL2 11 F3
South Hill, Hooe. PL9 18 C6
South Hill, Stoke. PL2 16 D2
South Milton St. PL4 18 B2
South View. PL5 8 B4
South View Clo. PL7 14 D2
South View Park. PL7 14 D2
South View Rd. PL9 20 A5
South View Ter. PL9 18 B1
Southern Clo. PL2 10 D1
Southern Ter. PL4 17 H1
Southernway. PL9 19 G4
Southgate Av. PL9 19 F6
Southgate Clo. PL9 19 F6
Southside St. PL1 3 C4
Southway Dri. PL6 4 B5
Southway La. PL6 5 E3
Southway La, Southway. PL6 4 A4
Southwell Rd. PL6 12 A1
Sovereign Ct. PL7 14 C4
Sparke Clo. PL7 15 G5
Speedwell Cres. PL6 12 C2
Speedwell Walk. PL6 12 D2
Spencer Rd. PL9 19 F3
Spire Ct. PL3 12 C3
Spring Park. PL6 5 H3
Springfield Av. PL9 19 H4
Springfield Clo. PL9 19 H4
Springfield Dri. PL3 11 F4
Springfield La. PL9 19 H4
Springfield Rise. PL9 19 H4
Springfield Rd. PL9 19 H5
Springhill. PL2 11 G1
Springhill Grn. PL2 11 G1
Springwood Clo. PL7 15 F6
Spruce Gdns. PL7 15 G4
Staddiscombe Rd. PL9 19 G6
Staddon Cres. PL9 19 F5
Staddon Grn. PL9 19 E5
Staddon La. PL9 18 B6
Staddon Park Rd. PL9 19 F5
Staddon Ter. PL1 3 A1
Stag La. PL9 20 A3
Stamford Clo. PL9 18 B5
*Stamford Fort Cotts, Stamford Rd. PL9 18 B5
Stamford La. PL9 18 B5
Stamford Rd. PL9 18 B5
Stanborough Rd. PL9 19 G4
Stanbury Av. PL6 8 B5
*Stanbury Ter, Laira Bridge Rd. PL4 18 C2
Standarhay. PL9 20 B4
Standarhay Clo. PL9 20 B4
Stangray Av. PL4 12 A1
Stanhope Rd. PL5 6 B5
Stanley Pl. PL4 18 C1
Stannary La. PL1 3 A1
Staple Clo. PL6 5 F2
Stapleford Gdns. PL5 7 E2
Station Rd, Elburton. PL9 20 B4
Station Rd, Keyham. PL2 10 D4

Station Rd, Plympton. PL7 14 D3
Station Rd, Tamerton Foliot. PL5 6 D1
Steeple Clo. PL9 19 G6
Steer Park Rd. PL7 15 H3
Stefan Clo. PL9 18 C6
Stenlake Pl. PL4 18 C1
Stenlake Ter. PL4 18 C1
Stentaway Clo. PL9 19 G3
Stentaway Dri. PL9 19 G3
Stentaway Rd. PL9 19 F4
Stephenson Way. PL5 7 E4
Stillman Ct. PL4 3 C4
Stillman St. PL4 3 C4
Stirling Ct. PL5 6 B5
*Stirling Pl, Stirling Rd. PL5 6 B5
Stirling Rd. PL5 6 B5
Stoggy La. PL7 15 F3
Stoke Rd. PL1 17 E3
Stokes La. PL1 3 C4
Stokesay Av. PL6 4 D5
Stokingway Clo. PL9 19 H6
Stone Barton Clo. PL7 14 C3
Stone Barton Rd. PL7 14 C3
Stonehouse Bri. PL1 16 D3
*Stonehouse Flats, Cremyll St. PL1 16 D4
Stonehouse St. PL1 16 D4
Stopford Pl. PL1 16 C2
Stott Clo. PL3 13 F4
Stour Clo. PL3 13 F3
Stowe Gdns. PL5 7 G4
Strand St. PL1 16 D4
Stratten Walk. PL2 11 H1
Strode Rd. PL7 15 E3
Stroma Clo. PL6 4 D3
Stroud Park Rd. PL2 11 H1
Stuart Rd. PL3 3 A1
Sturdee Rd. PL2 11 E4
Summerlands Clo. PL7 15 H4
*Summerlands Gdns, Summerlands Clo. PL7 15 H4
Summers Clo. PL6 12 D2
Sunderland Clo. PL9 18 C5
Sunny Dene. PL5 6 C5
Sunnyside Rd. PL4 18 C1
Sussex Pl. PL1 3 B4
Sussex Rd. PL2 10 D4
Sussex St. PL1 3 B4
Sussex Ter. PL2 10 D4
Sutherland Rd. PL4 3 C1
Sutton Pl. PL4 18 A2
Sutton Rd. PL4 4 D3
Swaindale Rd. PL3 12 A3
Swale Clo. PL3 12 D3
Swallows End. PL9 19 F3
Swan Gdns. PL7 15 E3
Swift Gdns. PL5 7 G5
Swinburne Gdns. PL5 7 G5
Sycamore Av. PL4 18 B2
Sycamore Dri. PL6 5 G3
Sycamore Way. PL6 9 G1
Sydney Clo. PL7 14 D4
Sydney St. PL1 3 A2

Tailyour Rd. PL6 8 C4
Talbot Gdns. PL5 10 B1
Tamar Av. PL2 10 D4
Tamar St. PL1 16 B2
Tamar Vs. PL9 19 E4
Tamar Way. PL5 7 F4
Tamar Wharf. PL1 10 C6
Tamerton Clo. PL5 6 C6
Tamerton Clo. PL5 7 F1
Tamerton Foliot Rd. PL6 8 A1
Tamerton Rd. PL6 5 F1
Tan St. PL7 15 E5
Tangmere Av. PL5 6 D1
Tapson Dri. PL9 18 B5
Taunton Av. PL5 7 F1
Taunton Pl. PL5 7 G1
Tavistock Pl. PL4 3 C2
Tavistock Rd. PL6 8 B6
*Tavy Ho, Duke St. PL1 16 B3
Tavy Pl. PL4 17 H1
Taw Clo. PL3 13 F3
Tay Gdns. PL3 13 E2
Teachers Clo. PL9 19 F5
Teats Hill Flats. PL4 17 H4
Teats Hill Rd. PL4 17 H4
Tees Clo. PL3 13 E2
Teign Rd. PL3 12 D3

Telford Cres. PL5 7 E5
Temeraire Rd. PL5 8 A5
Tenby Rd. PL5 6 B5
Tennyson Gdns. PL5 7 G5
Tern Gdns. PL7 15 E4
Terra Nova Grn. PL2 11 F4
Tewkesbury Clo. PL2 11 E1
Thackeray Gdns. PL5 7 G5
Thames Gdns. PL3 13 F4
The Arbour. PL6 4 C5
The Barbican. PL1 3 C4
*The Bridge, Custom Ho La. PL1 17 E5
The Broadway. PL9 19 F4
The Court. PL6 5 F4
The Crescent. PL1 3 A4
The Dell. PL3 14 B3
The Drive. PL3 12 A2
The Elms. PL3 16 D1
The Esplanade. PL1 3 A5
The Green. PL9 18 C5
The Grove, Plymstock. PL9 19 E3
The Grove, Stoke. PL3 16 D1
The Heathers. PL6 5 G3
The Hollows. PL9 19 H3
The Knoll. PL7 14 A3
The Lawns. PL5 8 B5
The Limes. PL6 8 C4
The Mead. PL1 14 C2
The Mews. PL1 16 C2
*The Narrows, Custom Ho La. PL1 17 E5
The Octagon. PL1 17 E3
*The Old Laundry, Craigie Dri. PL1 16 D3
The Old Wharf. PL9 18 C4
The Quay. PL1 18 C3
The Retreat. PL3 12 D2
The Spinney. PL7 15 G5
The Square. PL1 16 D3
The Terrace. PL1 16 A3
The Village. PL6 5 F6
Theatre Ope. PL1 16 C3
Therlow Rd. PL3 12 D3
Thetford Gdns. PL6 13 F1
Third Av, Billacombe. PL9 19 G2
Third Av, Stoke. PL1 16 D3
Third Av, Weston Mill. PL2 10 D2
Thirlmere Gdns. PL6 8 C2
Thistle Clo. PL6 5 H3
Thorn Hill Way. PL3 12 A3
Thorn Park. PL3 12 B4
Thornbury Pk Av. PL3 11 H3
Thornbury Rd. PL6 9 G2
Thornhill Rd. PL3 12 A3
Thornton Av. PL4 12 B6
Thornville Ter. PL4 18 D4
Thornyville Clo. PL9 18 D3
Thornyville Dri. PL9 18 D3
Thornyville Villas. PL9 18 D3
Thurlestone Walk. PL6 13 F1
Tillard Clo. PL7 15 H4
Tilly Clo. PL9 19 F6
Tin La. PL1 3 C4
Tin St. PL1 3 C4
Tintagel Cres. PL2 7 H6
Tintern Av. PL4 18 B2
Tithe Rd. PL7 14 A2
Tiverton Clo. PL6 5 F3
Tollox Pl. PL3 12 D5
Tor Clo. PL3 12 A2
Tor Cres. PL3 12 A2
Tor La. PL3 12 A2
Tor Rd. PL3 12 A2
Torbridge Rd. PL7 15 E2
Torbryan Clo. PL6 13 G1
Torland Rd. PL3 12 A4
Torr View Av. PL3 11 H2
Torridge Clo. PL7 15 F3
Torridge Clo. PL7 15 F3
Torridge Way. PL3 12 D4
Torver Clo. PL6 9 F4
Tory Way. PL7 14 D3
Torybrook Av. PL7 14 D3
*Torybrook Ct, Chamberlayne Dri. PL7 14 D3
Tothill Av. PL4 17 H3
Tothill La. PL4 18 A1
Tothill Rd. PL4 18 A1
Totnes Clo. PL7 15 H5
Towerfield Dri. PL6 5 G2
Towers Clo. PL6 9 H4

Townshend Av. PL2 10 D3
Tracey Ct. PL1 3 A2
Tracey St. PL1 3 A2
Trafalgar Clo. PL5 6 B6
Trafalgar Place La. PL1 16 C2
Trafalgar St. PL4 3 D3
Tramway Rd. PL6 5 H3
Transit Way. PL5 7 H4
Treago Clo. PL3 12 C2
Treago Gdns. PL6 5 F2
Treby Rd. PL7 15 F5
Trefusis Gdns. PL3 12 C5
Tregenna Clo. PL7 15 H5
Tregle Clo. PL6 5 G5
Trelawney Av. PL6 6 C6
Trelawney Pl. PL5 6 B6
Trelawney Rd. PL3 11 H4
Trelawney Rd La. PL3 11 H4
Trelawny Rd. PL7 14 C2
Treloweth Clo. PL2 11 H1
Trematon Ter. PL4 17 H1
*Trendlewood Rd,
  Meadowlands. PL6 5 G3
Trent Clo. PL3 12 D3
Trentham Clo. PL6 5 E4
Tresillian St. PL4 18 B2
Tresluggan Rd. PL5 6 C6
Tretower Clo. PL6 8 C1
Trevannion Clo. PL6 12 C1
Treveneague Gdns. PL2 11 H1
Treverbyn Rd. PL7 14 C3
Treverbyn Rd. PL7 14 D3
Trevessa Clo. PL2 11 H1
Trevithian Ter. PL2 11 F4
Trevithick Rd. PL5 6 D5
Trevone Gdns. PL2 8 A6
Trevose Way. PL3 13 E3
Trewithy Ct. PL6 8 C5
Trewithy Dri. PL6 8 C5
Trowbridge Clo. PL5 4 A6
Truro Dri. PL5 7 F1
Tucker Clo. PL9 10 D1
Tudor Clo. PL6 19 F6
Tunnel Cotts. PL6 9 H5
Turnbill Gdns. PL7 15 G4
Turnquay. PL9 18 C4
Turret Gro. PL2 12 B5
Tuxton Clo. PL7 15 H6
Tylney Clo. PL6 5 F4
Tyndale Clo. PL5 7 G5
Tything Walk. PL3 12 A3

Ullswater Cres. PL6 8 B2
Undercliff Rd. PL9 18 C4
Underhill Rd. PL3 16 D1
Underlane,
  Plympton. PL7 14 B4
Underlane,
  Plymstock. PL9 19 E5
Underley Clo. PL6 5 F4
Underwood. PL7 14 D5
*Underwood Cotts,
  Underwood Rd. PL7 14 C4
Underwood Rd. PL7 14 C4
Union Pl. PL1 17 E3
Union St. PL1 3 A4
Unity Clo. PL6 9 G1
Upland Dri. PL6 8 C1
Upper Knollys Ope Ter Sth.
  PL3 11 G5
Upper Knollys Ter La
  . PL3 11 G5
Upper Ridings. PL7 15 G2
Upton Clo. PL3 12 D2
Uxbridge Dri. PL5 6 D2

Vaagso Clo. PL1 16 B2
Valiant Av. PL5 7 E3
Valletort Clo. PL1 11 F6
Valletort La. PL1 11 F6
Valletort Pl. PL1 16 D3
Valletort Rd. PL1 16 D2
Valley Rd. PL7 14 B4
Valley View. PL6 5 H3
Valley View Clo. PL3 12 D3
Valley View Rd. PL3 12 D2
Valley Walk. PL6 9 H1
*Vanguard Ter,
  Saltash Rd. PL2 10 C3
Vapron Rd. PL3 12 A3
Vauban Pl. PL2 16 C1
Vaughan Clo. PL2 11 G2
Vauxhall Ct. PL4 3 C4
*Vauxhall Pl,
  Vauxhall St. PL4 3 C4
Vauxhall Quay. PL4 3 C4

Vauxhall St. PL4 3 C4
Venn Clo. PL3 12 A3
*Venn Ct,
  Venn Clo. PL3 12 A3
Venn Cres. PL3 12 A3
Venn Gdns. PL3 12 A2
Venn Gro. PL3 12 A2
*Venn La,
  Venn Clo. PL3 12 A3
Venn Way. PL3 12 A2
Vermont Gdns. PL2 10 D2
Verna Pl. PL5 6 C5
Verna Rd. PL2 6 D5
Vicarage Gdns. PL5 6 B5
Vicarage Rd. PL7 14 C3
Victoria Av. PL1 17 E2
*Victoria Cotts,
  Farm La. PL6 12 D1
*Victoria Cotts,
  George La. PL7 15 E4
Victoria Pl. PL2 16 C1
*Victoria Pl,
  Millbay Rd. PL1 3 A4
Victoria Rd. PL5 6 C5
Victoria Ter. PL4 3 C1
Victory St. PL2 10 C2
Village Dri. PL6 5 G1
Villiers Clo. PL9 19 E4
Vine Cres. PL2 11 F3
Vine Gdns. PL2 11 F3
Vinery La. PL9 20 B4
Vinstone Way. PL5 6 C6
Violet Dri. PL6 5 H2
Virginia Gdns. PL2 11 E2

Waddon Clo. PL7 15 E2
Wadham Ter. PL2 11 E4
Waggon Hill. PL7 15 F5
Wain Pk. PL7 15 F5
Wake St. PL4 3 A1
Wakefield Av. PL5 6 D5
Walcot Clo. PL6 9 G4
Waldon Clo. PL7 15 G3
Walker Ter. PL1 3 A5
Walkhampton Wk. PL6 9 G6
Wallace Rd. PL7 15 G5
Wallpark Clo. PL7 15 E2
Walnut Clo. PL7 15 G4
Walnut Dri. PL7 15 H4
Walnut Gdns. PL7 15 H4
Walsingham Ct. PL7 15 G3
Walters Rd. PL5 6 B5
Waltham Pl. PL2 11 E1
Walton Cres. PL5 7 H5
Wandle Pl. PL3 13 F4
Wanstead Gro. PL5 7 F4
Wantage Gdns. PL1 11 F6
Warburton Gdns. PL5 6 B6
Ward Pl. PL3 12 D4
Wardlow Clo. PL6 12 B1
Wardlow Gdns. PL6 12 B1
Wardour Walk. PL6 5 F3
Waring Rd. PL6 4 B3
Warleigh Av. PL2 10 D4
Warleigh Cres. PL6 4 C5
Warleigh Rd. PL4 17 G1
Warmwell Rd. PL5 6 D2
Warren Pk. PL6 5 G3
Warren St. PL2 16 B1
Warspite Gdns. PL5 8 A5
Warton Clo. PL5 8 A4
Warwick Av. PL5 8 A3
Warwick Orchard Clo.
  PL5 7 G4
Wasdale Clo. PL6 9 F4
Wasdale Gdns. PL6 9 F4
Washbourne Clo. PL1 10 C6
Waterloo Clo. PL1 16 D3
Waterloo Ct. PL1 16 D3
Waterloo St,
  Plymouth. PL4 3 D2
Waterloo St,
  Stoke. PL1 16 C2
Waterloo Yd. PL1 16 D2
Watson Gdns. PL4 18 A1
Watson Pl. PL4 18 B1
*Watts Cotts,
  Boringdon Rd. PL9 18 B4
Watts Park Rd. PL2 11 G2
Watts Rd. PL4 18 B1
Waveney Gdns. PL5 7 G4
Waverley Rd. PL5 6 C5
Waycott Walk. PL6 4 B4
Weir Clo. PL6 9 H4
Weir Gdns. PL6 9 H4
Weir Rd. PL6 9 H4

Welbeck Av. PL4 3 B1
Well Gdns. PL1 3 A2
Welland Gdns. PL3 12 D4
Wellfield Clo. PL7 15 H4
Wellhay Clo. PL9 20 B5
Wellington St,
  Plymouth. PL4 3 D2
Wellington St,
  Stoke. PL1 16 C2
Wellsbourne Pk. PL3 12 C3
Welsford Av. PL2 11 H4
Wembury Park Rd. PL3 11 H2
Wembury Rd. PL9 19 H5
Wenlock Gdns. PL2 11 F1
Wensum Clo. PL7 15 F4
Wentwood Gdns. PL6 9 G4
Wentwood Pl. PL6 9 G3
Wentworth Pl. PL2 18 B1
Wesley Av. PL3 12 A4
Wesley Pl,
  Mutley. PL4 12 A4
Wesley Pl, Stoke. PL2 16 C1
*Wesley Ter,
  Hyde Park Rd. PL3 12 A4
*Wesley Villas,
  Hyde Park Rd. PL3 12 A4
West Country Clo. PL2 10 D2
West Hill Rd. PL4 12 B5
West Hoe Rd. PL1 17 E4
West Malling Av. PL5 6 D2
West Park Dri. PL7 15 H4
West Park Hill. PL7 15 F2
Westbourne Rd. PL3 11 H4
*Westbury Ct,
  Fore St. PL1 16 B3
Westbury Ter. PL1 3 A2
Westcombe Cres. PL9 18 D6
Westcott Clo. PL6 12 C1
Westcroft Rd. PL5 6 C5
Westdown Rd. PL2 11 F3
Westeria Ter. PL2 11 G2
Western App. PL1 3 A3
Western College Rd.
  PL4 12 B4
Western Dri. PL3 12 D5
Western Wood Way.
  PL7 15 H4
Westfield. PL7 15 F3
Westfield Av. PL9 18 D5
Westhampnett Pl. PL5 7 E2
Westhays Clo. PL9 19 F6
Westmoor Clo. PL7 15 H3
Weston Mill Dri. PL5 10 C1
Weston Mill Hill. PL5 6 D6
Weston Mill La. PL5 7 F5
Weston Mill Rd. PL5 6 D5
Weston Park Rd. PL3 11 H3
Westways. PL9 18 C5
Westwood Av. PL6 9 F1
Wheatridge. PL7 14 B2
Whimple St. PL1 3 C4
Whin Bank Rd. PL5 8 A4
Whitby Cres. PL6 8 C5
Whitby Rd. PL6 8 D6
White Friars La. PL4 3 D3
White La. PL1 3 C5
Whitefield Ter. PL4 3 D2
Whiteford Rd. PL3 12 A3
Whitehall Dri. PL9 20 A4
Whitleigh Av. PL5 8 B4
*Whitleigh Cotts,
  Whitleigh Av. PL5 8 B4
Whitleigh Grn. PL5 7 H2
Whitleigh La. PL5 8 B4
*Whitleigh Villas,
  Whitleigh Av. PL5 8 B4
Whitleigh Way. PL5 7 H3
Whitsoncross La. PL5 4 A3
Whittington St. PL3 17 E2
Widewell La. PL6 5 F3
Widewell Rd. PL6 5 F3
Widey Ct. PL6 8 C5
Widey La. PL6 8 C5
*Widey Ter,
  Morshead Rd. PL6 8 B5
Widey Vw. PL3 12 B3
Wilderness Rd. PL3 12 A4
Wilkinson Rd. PL5 10 B1
William Evans Clo. PL6 4 B5
Williams Av. PL4 18 C2
Willow Clo. PL3 13 G3
Willow Cotts. PL7 14 D4
Willow Ct. PL6 13 G2
*Willow View Ter,
  Underwood Rd. PL7 14 C4
Willow Walk. PL6 9 G1

Wills Clo. PL6 4 C3
Wilmot Gdns. PL5 8 A4
Wilson Cres. PL2 11 F3
Wilton Rd. PL1 16 D2
Wilton St. PL1 17 E2
Wiltshire Clo. PL4 12 B5
Winchester Gdns. PL5 7 F2
Windermere Cres. PL6 8 C2
Windsor Pl. PL1 3 B4
Windsor Rd. PL3 12 D2
Windsor St. PL1 3 B4
Windsor Villas. PL1 3 B4
Wingfield Rd. PL3 16 D2
Wingfield Villas,
  Wingfield Rd. PL3 16 D2
Wingfield Way. PL3 17 E2
Winnicott Clo. PL6 4 C3
Winnow Clo. PL9 19 F6
Winsbury Ct. PL6 8 C5
Winstanley Walk. PL3 13 E3
Winston Av. PL4 3 B1
Witham Gdns. PL3 12 D4
Woburn Ter. PL9 18 D4
Wollaton Gro. PL5 7 E4
Wolridge Av. PL7 15 G4
Wolridge Way. PL7 15 G4
*Wolsdon Mews,
  Wolsdon St. PL1 17 E3
Wolsdon Pl. PL1 17 E3
Wolsdon St. PL1 17 E3
Wolseley Clo. PL1 11 E3
Wolseley Rd. PL2 6 A5
*Wolsley Ter, Houndiscombe
  Rd. PL4 3 C1
Wolverwood Clo. PL7 15 H6
Wolverwood La. PL7 15 E6
Wombwell Cres. PL2 10 C2
Wood Pk. PL6 9 H5
*Woodbine Cotts,
  Underwood Rd. PL7 14 C4
Woodbury Gdns. PL5 7 F3
Woodend Rd. PL6 5 G3
Woodford Av. PL7 14 A3
Woodford Clo. PL7 14 A2
Woodford Cres. PL7 14 A2
Woodford Grn. PL7 14 B2
Woodford Rd. PL6 5 G4
Woodford Ter. PL7 14 A3
Woodhey Rd. PL2 11 E2
Woodland Av. PL9 19 H3
Woodland Dri. PL7 15 H4
Woodland Rd. PL7 14 C3
Woodland Ter. PL4 3 D2
Woodland Ter La. PL4 12 B6
*Woodland Villas,
  Lipson Rd. PL4 3 D3
*Woodland Villas,
  Plymouth. PL7 14 A3
Woodlands. PL9 19 G5
Woodlands La. PL6 9 H5
Woodside La. PL4 12 B6
Woodside Av. PL9 18 D5
Woodside Ct. PL7 14 D5
Woodstock Gdns. PL5 6 C5
Woodview. PL9 19 H5
Woodview Park. PL9 19 H5
Woodville Clo. PL2 10 D2
Woodville Rd. PL2 11 E3
Woodway. PL9 19 G4
Woollcombe Av. PL7 15 F5
*Woolster Ct,
  Vauxhall St. PL4 3 C4
Woolwell Cres. PL6 5 G2
Woolwell Dri. PL6 5 G2
Woolwell Rd. PL6 5 G2
Wordsworth Cres. PL2 10 D2
Wordsworth Rd. PL2 10 D2
Wren Gdns. PL7 14 C3
Wrens Gate. PL9 19 F3
Wright Clo. PL1 10 C6
Wycliffe Rd. PL3 12 D5
Wye Gdns. PL3 13 F2
Wykeham Dri. PL2 11 E1
Wyndham La. PL1 17 E3
*Wyndham Pl,
  Stoke. PL1 17 E3
Wyndham Sq. PL1 17 E3
Wyndham St East. PL1 17 F3
Wyndham St West. PL1 17 E3
Wyoming Clo. PL3 12 D4
Wythburn Gdns. PL6 9 G4

Yardley Gdns. PL6 9 G3
Yarrow Mead. PL9 20 C4
Yarrowpoole Cotts.
  PL9 20 D4

Yealmpstone Clo. PL7 15 G5
Yealmpstone Dri. PL7 15 G5
Yeats Clo. PL5 7 H4
Yelverton Clo. PL5 6 D3
*Yelverton Ter,
  North Rd East. PL4 3 B1
Yeo Clo. PL3 12 D4
Yeomans Way. PL7 15 F5
Yewdale Gdns. PL6 9 F4
Yonder St. PL9 18 C5
York Pl. PL2 16 C1
York Rd. PL5 10 C1
York St. PL1 16 D4
York Ter. PL2 10 D4

Zion St. PL1 3 B4

## IVYBRIDGE

Abbot Rd. PL21 25 A2
Acland Rd. PL21 25 A2
Ash Gro. PL21 25 E3
Badgers Clo. PL21 25 A3
Barn Clo. PL21 25 A2
Barons Pyke. PL21 25 E3
Beacon Clo. PL21 25 C2
Beacon Rd. PL21 25 C2
Belmont Rd. PL21 25 C3
Berkeley Way. PL21 25 D4
Bishops Clo. PL21 25 E2
Blachford Rd. PL21 25 C2
Blackett Clo. PL21 25 D3
Blackthorn Dri. PL21 25 D3
Blair Rd. PL21 25 D3
Bridge Pk. PL21 25 D2
Brook Rd. PL21 25 D2
Brunel Way. PL21 25 D2
Buckfast Clo. PL21 25 D3
Buddle Clo. PL21 25 E2
Burlingdon Pk. PL21 25 A3
Butterdon Walk. PL21 25 E3
Cameron Dri. PL21 25 A3
Canterbury Clo. PL21 25 D4
Carter Rd. PL21 25 D2
*Causeway Cotts,
  Woodland Rd. PL21 25 A3
Chapel Pl. PL21 25 C3
Charles Hankin Way.
  PL21 25 E3
Charlton Ter. PL21 25 D2
Church Meadow. PL21 25 A3
Clare St. PL21 25 C3
Claymans Pathway.
  PL21 25 A2
Cleeve Dri. PL21 25 B3
*Cleveland Pl,
  Western Rd. PL21 25 B3
Cole La. PL21 25 D2
Corfe Clo. PL21 25 D4
Cornwood Rd. PL21 25 A2
Costly St. PL21 25 D3
Crescent Gdns. PL21 25 C2
Crescent Rd. PL21 25 C2
Crestfield Rise. PL21 25 B3
Cursons Way. PL21 25 A2
Dairy La. PL21 25 D3
Dairy Rd. PL21 25 D3
Deer Park. PL21 25 E3
Delamore Clo. PL21 25 A3
Donkey La. PL21 25 C3
Douro St. PL21 25 D3
Drovers Way. PL21 25 A2
Dunsterville. PL21 25 E2
Eden Cotts. PL21 25 D2
Elizabeth Clo. PL21 25 E2
Endsleigh View. PL21 25 A3
Erme Ct. PL21 25 D3
Erme Dri. PL21 25 C3
Erme Rd. PL21 25 C3
Exeter Rd. PL21 25 D3
Fairway Av. PL21 25 B3
Fernbank Av. PL21 25 A1
Fernhill Clo. PL21 25 E3
Filham Manor Clo. PL21 25 D3
Filham Moor La. PL21 25 D3
Fincer Dri. PL21 25 A2
Firtree Rise. PL21 25 D3
*Flora Cotts,
  Woodland Rd. PL21 25 A3
Ford Clo. PL21 25 A2
Fore St. PL21 25 C3
Glanvilles Rd. PL21 25 C3
Godwell La. PL21 25 F3

Gorse Way. PL21 25 D3
Greenfield Dri. PL21 25 C3
Greenway Clo. PL21 25 C3
Greenwood Clo. PL21 25 C3
Harford Rd. PL21 25 D2
*Harris Cotts,
　Fore St. PL21 25 C3
Hartley Ct. PL21 25 C3
Haytor Dri. PL21 25 D3
Heather Walk. PL21 25 D3
Henlake Clo. PL21 25 B2
High Acre Dri. PL21 25 A2
Higher Brook Pk. PL21 25 A3
Highland St. PL21 25 C3
Holman Way. PL21 25 A2
Holtwood Dri. PL21 25 A3
Howards Way. PL21 25 A1
Hunters Clo. PL21 25 B2
INDUSTRIAL & RETAIL:
　Stowford Business
　Park. PL21 25 D3
　Westover Ind Est.
　PL21 25 B4
Ivybridge By-Pass.
　PL21 25 C4
Ivydene Rd. PL21 25 B3
Jubilee Clo. PL21 25 E2
Julian Rd. PL21 25 B3
Keaton Rd. PL21 25 C3
Kennel La. PL21 25 A3
*Kimberley Ct,
　Fore St. PL21 25 C3
Kimberley Villas. PL21 25 B3
Langham Levels. PL21 25 A2
Langham Way. PL21 25 B3
Leland Gro. PL21 25 C4
Leonards Rd. PL21 25 D3
Longbrook Rd. PL21 25 A3
Lower Brook Pk. PL21 25 A3
Luscombe Clo. PL21 25 A3
Lydford Clo. PL21 25 D4
McAndrew Walk. PL21 25 E2
Mallet Rd. PL21 25 A2
Manor Clo. PL21 25 C3
Manor Dri. PL21 25 B3
Manor Way. PL21 25 C3
Marjorie Kelly Way.
　PL21 25 C3
Marshall Dri. PL21 25 C4
Maton Clo. PL21 25 D3
Mayfield. PL21 25 A3
Mead Clo. PL21 25 A2
Meatherel Clo. PL21 25 B3
Mill La. PL21 25 D1
Mill Meadow. PL21 25 D2
*Moorview Villas,
　Western Rd. PL21 25 B3
New Meadow. PL21 25 A2
Nirvana Clo. PL21 25 C2
Oak Gdns. PL21 25 E3
Oaktree Clo. PL21 25 A2
*Oate Villas,
　Western Rd. PL21 25 B3
Okehampton Way.
　PL21 25 D4
Orchard Ct. PL21 25 B3
Orchid Av. PL21 25 A2
Paddock Dri. PL21 25 C3
Pallace La. PL21 25 F2
Paper Makers La. PL21 25 C2
Park Clo. PL21 25 C2
Park St. PL21 25 C3
Parkside. PL21 25 E3
Pinehurst Way. PL21 25 A2
Plover Rise. PL21 25 A2
Portal Pl. PL21 25 B3
Pound Farm La. PL21 25 C3
Prideaux Rd. PL21 25 E2
Primrose Clo. PL21 25 D3
Primrose Mdw. PL21 25 A2
Priory Clo. PL21 25 B2
Pykes Down. PL21 25 E3
Raleigh Rd. PL21 25 A2
Rivers Clo. PL21 25 E3
*Rockhill Villas,
　Western Rd. PL21 25 B3
Rue St Pierre. PL21 25 E3
St Austin Clo. PL21 25 B2
St Johns Clo. PL21 25 B3
St Johns Rd. PL21 25 B3
St Peters Way. PL21 25 E3
Sandy La. PL21 25 D2
Savery Clo. PL21 25 E2
Sedge Clo. PL21 25 D3
Sherwell Hill. PL21 25 F4
Sherwill Clo. PL21 25 A2

Slipperstone Dri. PL21 25 A1
Speakers Rd. PL21 25 E2
Springwood Clo. PL21 25 E2
Staniforth Dri. PL21 25 D4
Stannary Clo. PL21 25 E2
Station Rd. PL21 25 C2
Stonehedge Clo. PL21 25 D3
Summerfield Ct. PL21 25 A2
The Chase. PL21 25 D4
The Coppice. PL21 25 A3
The Groves. PL21 25 C2
The Kennels. PL21 25 B2
The Pippins. PL21 25 A3
The Spinney. PL21 25 A3
Toll Bar. PL21 25 E2
Tom Maddock Gdns.
　PL21 25 E3
Toms Clo. PL21 25 A2
Torre Clo. PL21 25 F3
Trehill Rd. PL21 25 D3
Trematon Dri. PL21 25 D3
Trinnaman Clo. PL21 25 D3
Trumpers Clo. PL21 25 A3
Two Moors Way. PL21 25 E1
Uphill Clo. PL21 25 E3
Waltham Clo. PL21 25 D4
Waterside. PL21 25 C3
Waterslade Dri. PL21 25 C3
Wayside. PL21 25 B3
Weatherdon Dri. PL21 25 E2
Wellstones Clo. PL21 25 E3
Western Rd. PL21 25 B3
Westover Clo. PL21 25 B3
*Westover La,
　Woodlands. PL21 25 B3
Widdicombe Dri. PL21 25 D3
Windsor Clo. PL21 25 D4
Wood Park. PL21 25 D2
Woodburn Clo. PL21 25 D3
Woodfield Cres. PL21 25 E3
Woodland Dri. PL21 25 B3
Woodland Rd. PL21 25 A3
Woodland Ter. PL21 25 B3
Woodlands. PL21 25 B3
Woodside Clo. PL21 25 C3
Woolcombe La. PL21 25 D4
Woolms Mdw. PL21 25 A3
Worthele Clo. PL21 25 D3
Yeolland La. PL21 25 D3
Yeolland Pk. PL21 25 D3
Zeth Hill La. PL21 25 A1
Zion Pl. PL21 25 C3

## MILLBROOK

Anderton Rise. PL10 24 B3
Armada Rd. PL10 24 C6
Barton Mews. PL10 24 B1
Blindwell Hill. PL10 24 B2
Calvez Clo. PL10 24 C1
Camperknowle Clo.
　PL10 24 C1
Cawsand Park. PL10 24 C5
Coombe Park. PL10 24 C5
Coombe Park Clo. PL10 24 C5
Devonport Hill. PL10 24 D5
Earles Dri. PL10 24 B1
Edgcumbe Cres. PL10 24 C1
Egret Clo. PL10 24 C1
Forder Hill. PL10 24 B6
Forder La. PL10 24 C6
Fore St,
　Kingsand. PL10 24 D5
Fore St,
　Millbrook. PL10 24 B2
Garrett St. PL10 24 D6
Green Pk. PL10 24 C5
Greenland. PL10 24 B2
Hat La. PL10 24 B6
Heavitree Rd. PL10 24 D5
Heron Clo. PL10 24 C1
Higher Anderton Rd.
　PL10 24 B2
Hounster Dri. PL10 24 A3
Insworke Clo. PL10 24 C1
Insworke Cres. PL10 24 C1
Insworke Pl. PL10 24 B2
Jackmans Mdw. PL10 24 C4
King St. PL10 24 B2
Knill Cross. PL10 24 B2
Little La. PL10 24 B2
Little Point Cres. PL10 24 C2
Lower Anderton Rd.
　PL10 24 B2

Lower Row. PL10 24 D5
Maker La. PL10 24 B2
Market St. PL10 24 D6
Millpool Head. PL10 24 B2
Millpool Rd. PL10 24 C1
Millview Gdns. PL10 24 B2
Millview Rd. PL10 24 B2
Molesworth Ter. PL10 24 C5
New Rd. PL10 24 C6
New Rd Clo. PL10 24 C5
New St. PL10 24 B2
Newport St. PL10 24 B2
Pier La. PL10 24 D6
Radford La. PL10 24 A3
St Andrews Pl. PL10 24 C6
St Andrews St,
　Cawsand. PL10 24 C6
St Andrews St,
　Millbrook. PL10 24 A2
St Johns Clo. PL10 24 B2
St Johns Rd. PL10 24 A1
Sango St. PL10 24 B1
Southdown Rd. PL10 24 C1
Speedwell Clo. PL10 24 B2
*The Bound,
　The Square. PL10 24 D6
The Cleave. PL10 24 D5
The Drive. PL10 24 D5
The Green. PL10 24 D5
The Parade. PL10 24 B2
The Square. PL10 24 D6
Trencher La. PL10 24 A5
Wells Ct. PL10 24 A3
Welman Rd. PL10 24 C1
West St. PL10 24 A3
Woodcock Clo. PL10 24 C1

## NEWTON FERRERS

Beacon Hill. PL8 21 B4
Church Park. PL8 21 D5
Church Park Rd. PL8 21 D5
Cottage Grn. PL8 21 D4
Court Rd. PL8 21 A4
Court Wood. PL8 21 A5
Dillons. PL8 21 D4
Lower Court Rd. PL8 21 A4
Meadow Clo. PL8 21 D4
Middle Leigh. PL8 21 B4
Newton Clo. PL8 21 D5
Newton Hill. PL8 21 C5
Parsonage Rd. PL8 21 D4
Passage Wood Rd. PL8 21 B6
Pillory Hill. PL8 21 C6
Revelstoke Rd. PL8 21 D6
Riverside Rd East. PL8 21 D5
Riverside Rd West. PL8 21 B5
St Catherines. PL8 21 D4
Stoke Rd. PL8 21 D6
The Fairway. PL8 21 C4
The Foss. PL8 21 C6
The Green. PL8 21 D4
The Oaks. PL8 21 A4
Wrights La. PL8 21 C5
Yealm Rd. PL8 21 D5
Yealm View Rd. PL8 21 D5

## SALTASH

Adit La. PL12 22 C3
Alamein Ct. PL12 22 C3
Alamein Rd. PL12 22 C3
Albert Rd. PL12 22 E3
Alexandra Sq. PL12 22 E3
Ashbirch Parc. PL12 22 A2
Babis Farm Ct. PL12 22 D3
Babis Farm Way. PL12 22 D3
Babis La. PL12 22 E4
Back Hill. PL12 22 B3
Barkers Hill. PL12 22 B3
Barn Park. PL12 22 D2
Barrow Down. PL12 22 A2
Beatrice Av. PL12 22 C3
Beaumont Ter. PL12 22 E1
Belle Vue Rd. PL12 22 E2
Beweys Park. PL12 22 B2
Birkdale Clo. PL12 22 B3
Biscombe Gdns. PL12 22 E2
*Boscundle Row,
　Fore St. PL12 22 E3
Briansway. PL12 22 B3

Broad Walk. PL12 22 C3
Brookdown Ter. PL12 22 D2
Brooking Way. PL12 22 B2
Brooks Hill. PL12 22 D1
Broom Hill. PL12 22 B3
Brunel Rd. PL12 22 B1
Buller Park. PL12 22 B2
Burnett Clo. PL12 22 B3
Burraton Rd. PL12 22 A1
Burry Park. PL12 22 B2
Butterdown. PL12 22 A2
Cabot Clo. PL12 22 D3
Callington Rd. PL12 22 B1
Caradan Ter. PL12 22 D2
Carew Gdns. PL12 22 B2
Carey Ct. PL12 22 C1
Carnoustie Dri. PL12 22 B3
Carrisbrooke Way.
　PL12 22 A2
Castle Ct. PL12 22 A3
Castle Rise. PL12 22 B4
Castle View. PL12 22 B4
Castlemead Clo. PL12 22 C2
Castlemead Dri. PL12 22 B2
Cedar Ct. PL12 22 E2
Channon Rd. PL12 22 B1
Chapel Rd. PL12 22 A2
Chapman Ct. PL12 22 A2
Chichester Cres. PL12 22 D3
Church Rd. PL12 22 C3
Churchill Walk. PL12 22 D4
Churchtown Vale. PL12 22 B3
Clear View. PL12 22 C2
Convent Clo. PL12 22 D2
Cook Ct. PL12 22 A2
Coombe Park. PL12 22 E3
Coombe Rd. PL12 22 E3
Courtlands. PL12 22 C4
Cowdray Clo. PL12 22 D3
Culver Rd. PL12 22 E3
Dane Ct. PL12 22 E2
Daws Ct. PL12 22 E3
Deacon Clo. PL12 22 E4
Deacon Dri. PL12 22 E4
Deer Park. PL12 22 D2
Down Clo. PL12 22 B3
Drakefield Dri. PL12 22 E2
Dunheved Rd. PL12 22 D3
Edwards Cres. PL12 22 A3
Elliott Clo. PL12 22 C3
Ellwell Rd. PL12 22 E2
Essa Rd. PL12 22 D3
Fairmead Mews. PL12 22 A2
Fairmead Rd. PL12 22 B2
Fairway. PL12 22 B3
Farm La. PL12 22 B4
Fenten Pk. PL12 22 D2
Fernside Way. PL12 22 B2
Fore St. PL12 22 E3
Forge La. PL12 22 A1
Forsythia Dri. PL12 22 A2
Foxglove Way. PL12 22 A2
Frith Rd. PL12 22 C2
Frobisher Dri. PL12 22 D3
Gallacher Way. PL12 22 A2
Gilston Rd. PL12 22 B1
Glanville Ter. PL12 22 E2
Glebe Av. PL12 22 D2
Gordon Ct. PL12 22 C3
Greenfield Rd. PL12 22 B3
Grenfell Av. PL12 22 B2
Hallett Clo. PL12 22 A2
Hardings Clo. PL12 22 C1
Hawks Pk. PL12 22 A3
Hawthorns. PL12 22 C3
Hearl Rd. PL12 22 A2
Hessary Vw. PL12 22 D1
Hewitt Clo. PL12 22 B3
Higher Port View. PL12 22 D3
Highfield Rd. PL12 22 D2
Hillside Av. PL12 22 E2
Hillside Rd. PL12 22 D2
Hobbs Cres. PL12 22 B2
Hodge Clo. PL12 22 B3
Holcroft Clo. PL12 22 E2
Home Park Rd. PL12 22 E2
Homer Pk. PL12 22 C2
INDUSTRIAL & RETAIL:
　Gwel-Avon Business Pk.
　PL12 22 C1
　Moorlands Trading Est.
　PL12 22 A1
　Saltash Business Pk.
　PL12 22 A1

Saltash Ind Est. PL12 22 B1
Saltash Parkway
　Ind Est. PL12 22 A1
Jackson Way. PL12 22 D2
Jubilee. PL12 22 C2
Kerswick Ct. PL12 22 C1
Killigrew Av. PL12 22 C4
King Edward Rd. PL12 22 D3
Lander Rd. PL12 22 E2
Langerwell Clo. PL12 22 A2
Langerwell La. PL12 22 A2
Larch Clo. PL12 22 A2
Lean Way. PL12 22 D3
Leat View. PL12 22 A2
Linnet Ct. PL12 22 A3
Liskeard Rd. PL12 22 A2
Lollabury Rd. PL12 22 C2
Long Acre. PL12 22 A1
Long Park Rd. PL12 22 C3
Longmeadow Rd. PL12 22 D2
Longview Rd. PL12 22 C2
Love La. PL12 22 D3
Lower Fore St. PL12 22 E3
Lower Port View. PL12 22 E3
Lynher Dri. PL12 22 D4
Manor Park. PL12 22 C3
Marlborough Clo. PL12 22 D3
Maybrook Dri. PL12 22 B3
Meadowsweet Pk. PL12 22 A3
Meadway. PL12 22 C4
Middlefield Clo. PL12 22 A2
Montgomery Clo. PL12 22 C2
Moorland Vw. PL12 22 E1
Moorlands La. PL12 22 B1
Mortimore Clo. PL12 22 A2
Mote Park. PL12 22 A2
Mulberry Rd. PL12 22 C3
New Rd. PL12 22 B2
Newman Rd. PL12 22 E2
Nilch Pk. PL12 22 A2
North Rd. PL12 22 E2
Oaklands Dri. PL12 22 B2
Oaklands Grn. PL12 22 B2
Old Ferry Rd. PL12 22 E2
Parkesway. PL12 22 C3
Pill La. PL12 22 D1
Plougastel Dri. PL12 22 D2
Plough Green. PL12 22 A2
Ploughboy Mews. PL12 22 A2
Pollard Clo. PL12 22 A3
Pollards Way. PL12 22 C1
Pondfield Rd. PL12 22 B2
Porter Way. PL12 22 B2
Pounds Park. PL12 22 E2
Prospect La. PL12 22 A2
Prospect Walk. PL12 22 A2
Prouse Rise. PL12 22 D3
Rashleigh Alley. PL12 22 C4
Ridgeway. PL12 22 C4
River View. PL12 22 E1
Rowan Ct. PL12 22 A3
Russell Clo. PL12 22 B2
Rye Hill. PL12 22 A3
St Andrews Clo. PL12 22 B3
St Annes Rd. PL12 22 C2
St Georges Rd. PL12 22 C2
St Stephens Hill. PL12 22 B4
St Stephens Rd. PL12 22 B3
Saltash By-Pass. PL12 22 A1
Saltmill La. PL12 22 D1
Sandquay La. PL12 22 E2
Sleep Clo. PL12 22 A2
Smithfield Dri. PL12 22 A2
Smiths Way. PL12 22 A2
Smithys Clo. PL12 22 B1
Snell Dri. PL12 22 B2
Southfield. PL12 22 B2
Spencer Gdns. PL12 22 D3
Spire Hill Pk. PL12 22 C3
Stanlake Clo. PL12 22 C3
Station Rd. PL12 22 E3
Summerfields. PL12 22 B4
Sunningdale Rd. PL12 22 B3
Sycamore Rd. PL12 22 A2
Tamar Bridge. PL12 22 F3
Tamar St. PL12 22 F3
Tamar Vw. PL12 22 E4
Tannery Ct. PL12 22 B3
Tavy Rd. PL12 22 C2
Taylor Clo. PL12 22 B2
Taylor Rd. PL12 22 B2
The Bridges. PL12 22 F
The Brook. PL12
The Close. PL12
The Court. PL12
The Green. Pl 1

| | | | |
|---|---|---|---|
| The Hedgerows. PL12 | 22 A2 | Cedar Dri. PL11 | 23 A2 |
| The Keep. PL12 | 22 A2 | Chapel Row. PL11 | 23 E2 |
| The Rivers. PL12 | 22 D4 | Chapeldown Rd. PL11 | 23 C3 |
| The Speares. PL12 | 22 A3 | Chestnut Clo. PL11 | 23 B2 |
| The Square. PL12 | 22 A2 | Clarence Rd. PL11 | 23 D1 |
| Thorn La. PL12 | 22 B2 | Clegg Av. PL11 | 23 A1 |
| Tincombe Rd. PL12 | 22 B3 | Colwyn Rd. PL11 | 23 C2 |
| Tobruk Rd. PL12 | 22 C2 | Cremyll Rd. PL11 | 23 D3 |
| Torbridge Clo. PL12 | 22 B2 | Davy Clo. PL11 | 23 A1 |
| Tower Ct. PL12 | 22 A3 | Evenden Ct. PL11 | 23 C1 |
| Tower View. PL12 | 22 C4 | Ferry St. PL11 | 23 F2 |
| Trelawney Rd. PL12 | 22 D3 | Fistral Clo. PL11 | 23 A1 |
| Two Hills Pk. PL12 | 22 A3 | Fore St. PL11 | 23 E2 |
| Uplands. PL12 | 22 C4 | Goad Av. PL11 | 23 A2 |
| Valley Rd. PL12 | 22 D3 | Goad Clo. PL11 | 23 A2 |
| Victoria Rd. PL12 | 22 E3 | Gordon Ter. PL11 | 23 D3 |
| Vincent Way. PL12 | 22 C2 | Gravesend Gdns. PL11 | 23 E1 |
| Warfelton Cres. PL12 | 22 C3 | Gurney Clo. PL11 | 23 A2 |
| Warfelton Gdns. PL12 | 22 C3 | Gwithian Clo. PL11 | 23 A1 |
| Warraton Clo. PL12 | 22 C2 | Hamoaze Rd. PL11 | 23 E3 |
| Warraton Rd. PL12 | 22 C2 | Harbour St. PL11 | 23 E2 |
| Wentworth Rd. PL12 | 22 B3 | Harvey St. PL11 | 23 E2 |
| Wesley Rd. PL12 | 22 E3 | Hawthorn Av. PL11 | 23 A2 |
| Westbourne Ter. PL12 | 22 E3 | Ince Clo. PL11 | 23 A1 |
| Willow Grn. PL12 | 22 B3 | Jago Av. PL11 | 23 D2 |
| Windmill Hill. PL12 | 22 D3 | Kempton Ter. PL11 | 23 D2 |
| Windsor La. PL12 | 22 D3 | Khyber Clo. PL11 | 23 C2 |
| Wood Acre. PL12 | 22 A1 | King St. PL11 | 23 F2 |
| Wood Clo. PL12 | 22 A2 | Kingsley Av. PL11 | 23 D3 |
| Yellowtor Ct. PL12 | 22 A3 | Liscawn Ter. PL11 | 23 D2 |
| Yellowtor Rd. PL12 | 22 A3 | Macey St. PL11 | 23 E1 |

## TORPOINT

| | | | |
|---|---|---|---|
| Adams Clo. PL11 | 23 A2 | Maker Rd. PL11 | 23 C3 |
| Adams Cres. PL11 | 23 A2 | Maple Av. PL11 | 23 B2 |
| Adela Rd. PL11 | 23 C1 | Marine Ct. PL11 | 23 D3 |
| Albion Bungalows. | | Marine Dri. PL11 | 23 E3 |
| PL11 | 23 D1 | Mill La. PL11 | 23 C2 |
| Albion Ct. PL11 | 23 E1 | Millhouse Park. PL11 | 23 C3 |
| Albion Rd. PL11 | 23 D1 | Moorview. PL11 | 23 D1 |
| Alexandra Ter. PL11 | 23 E3 | Mount Edgcumbe Ter. | |
| Antony Rd. PL11 | 23 C1 | PL11 | 23 D3 |
| *Arthur Ter, | | Mullion Clo. PL11 | 23 A1 |
| Bellevue Sq. PL11 | 23 E2 | Murdock Rd. PL11 | 23 A2 |
| Barossa Rd. PL11 | 23 E2 | Navy Ter. PL11 | 23 E3 |
| Beech Clo. PL11 | 23 C2 | Nelson St. PL11 | 23 E2 |
| Bellevue Sq. PL11 | 23 E2 | North Rd. PL11 | 23 D3 |
| Bickern Rd. PL11 | 23 E2 | Park Rd. PL11 | 23 D2 |
| Buller Clo. PL11 | 23 D2 | Peacock Av. PL11 | 23 C2 |
| Buller Rd. PL11 | 23 D2 | Pendennis Clo. PL11 | 23 A1 |
| Carbeile Rd. PL11 | 23 C2 | Pendilly Av. PL11 | 23 A3 |
| Carew Ter. PL11 | 23 E3 | Quarry St. PL11 | 23 E2 |
| Carlyon Clo. PL11 | 22 A1 | Roberts Av. PL11 | 23 D2 |
| Cedar Clo. PL11 | 23 A2 | Roeselare Av. PL11 | 23 C2 |
| | | Roeselare Clo. PL11 | 23 C1 |
| | | Rowe St. PL11 | 23 E2 |
| | | St James St. PL11 | 23 E2 |

| | | | |
|---|---|---|---|
| Salamanca St. PL11 | 23 E2 | Pump Hill. PL9 | 26 A2 |
| Sango Rd. PL11 | 23 C3 | Rose Hill. PL9 | 26 C2 |
| Sconner Rd. PL11 | 23 D2 | Ryeland Clo. PL9 | 26 C1 |
| Sennen Clo. PL11 | 23 A1 | St Werburgh Clo. PL9 | 26 C2 |
| Sycamore Dri. PL11 | 23 B2 | Seaview Dri. PL9 | 26 C2 |
| Sydney Rd. PL11 | 23 D1 | Southland Pk Cres. PL9 | 26 B2 |
| Tamar St. PL11 | 23 E2 | Southland Pk Rd. PL9 | 26 A3 |
| Thanckes Clo. PL11 | 23 C1 | Traine Rd. PL9 | 26 C1 |
| Thanckes Dri. PL11 | 23 C1 | Upland Gdns. PL9 | 26 D1 |
| The Lawns. PL11 | 23 C1 | Valley Dri. PL9 | 26 C2 |
| The Mews. PL11 | 23 C2 | Veasypark. PL9 | 26 C2 |
| Tregoning Rd. PL11 | 23 A2 | Warren Clo. PL9 | 26 C2 |
| Trelawney Rise. PL11 | 23 A2 | Warren La. PL9 | 26 D2 |
| Trengrouse Av. PL11 | 23 A2 | Wembury Mdws. PL9 | 26 C1 |
| Trevel View. PL11 | 23 C2 | | |
| Trevithick Av. PL11 | 23 A1 | | |
| Trevol Rd. PL11 | 23 A2 | | |

### YEALMPTON

| | | | |
|---|---|---|---|
| Trevorder Clo. PL11 | 23 B3 | | |
| Trevorder Rd. PL11 | 23 A2 | | |
| Vicarage Rd. PL11 | 23 D2 | Boldventure. PL8 | 21 B2 |
| Victoria St. PL11 | 23 D2 | Bowden Farm. PL8 | 21 B1 |
| Well Park Rd. PL11 | 23 D1 | Bowden Hill. PL8 | 21 B1 |
| Wellington St. PL11 | 23 E2 | Chapel Rd. PL8 | 21 C2 |
| Westlake Clo. PL11 | 23 A2 | Church Clo. PL8 | 21 B2 |
| Windsor Ter. PL11 | 23 F2 | Church La. PL8 | 21 B2 |
| Woodland Way. PL11 | 23 B1 | Church Park Rd. PL8 | 21 C3 |
| York Rd. PL11 | 23 D2 | Churchway. PL8 | 21 B2 |
| | | Creamery Clo. PL8 | 21 B3 |
| | | Dixon Ter. PL8 | 21 B3 |
| | | Elm Tree Clo. PL8 | 21 C1 |

## WEMBURY

| | | | |
|---|---|---|---|
| | | Elm Tree Park. PL8 | 21 C1 |
| Adams La. PL9 | 26 A1 | Ford Rd. PL8 | 21 C2 |
| Barton La. PL9 | 26 C1 | Fore St. PL8 | 21 B1 |
| Beach Rd. PL9 | 26 B3 | Hearn La. PL8 | 21 C1 |
| Beach View Cres. PL9 | 26 B2 | Hillside. PL8 | 21 C3 |
| Brownhill La. PL9 | 26 C2 | Hillside Dri. PL8 | 21 C3 |
| Church Rd. PL9 | 26 B2 | Hillside Way. PL8 | 21 C3 |
| Cliff Rd. PL9 | 26 B3 | Marjory Walk. PL8 | 21 A2 |
| Colliers Clo. PL9 | 26 C2 | Market St. PL8 | 21 C1 |
| Cory Ct. PL9 | 26 D1 | Milizac Clo. PL8 | 21 A2 |
| Cross Park Rd. PL9 | 26 C1 | New Rd. PL8 | 21 C2 |
| Crossways. PL9 | 26 C2 | Orchard Clo. PL8 | 21 C2 |
| Ford Rd. PL9 | 26 A1 | Ploughman Way. PL8 | 21 C2 |
| Hawthorn Dri. PL9 | 26 B3 | Riverside Walk. PL8 | 21 C2 |
| Hawthorn Pk Rd. PL9 | 26 B3 | Rockdale Rd. PL8 | 21 C3 |
| Highfield Dri. PL9 | 26 C1 | Rounds Nest. PL8 | 21 C3 |
| Hillcrest Clo. PL9 | 26 C2 | Stray Park. PL8 | 21 B2 |
| **INDUSTRIAL & RETAIL:** | | Sunnyside. PL8 | 21 B1 |
| Knighton Hill Business | | The Borough. PL8 | 21 C2 |
| Centre. PL9 | 26 D1 | Torr Bridge Park. PL8 | 21 C2 |
| Knighton Hill. PL9 | 26 D1 | Torr Hill. PL8 | 21 C2 |
| Knighton Rd. PL9 | 26 C1 | Torr La. PL8 | 21 C3 |
| Laburnum Dri. PL9 | 26 C2 | Torre Cotts. PL8 | 21 C3 |
| Leyford Clo. PL9 | 26 C2 | Tuckers Clo. PL8 | 21 C2 |
| Mewstone Av. PL9 | 26 C2 | Underhay. PL8 | 21 A2 |
| Mount Pleasant. PL9 | 26 A1 | Waltacre. PL8 | 21 B3 |
| | | West Park. PL8 | 21 C3 |

| | |
|---|---|
| Yealmbury Hill. PL8 | 21 C1 |
| Yealmbury Villas. PL8 | 21 C1 |
| Yealmpton Park. PL8 | 21 A2 |

## YELVERTON

| | |
|---|---|
| Beech View Av. PL20 | 26 B4 |
| *Beech Villas, | |
| The Green, PL20 | 26 B5 |
| Binkham Hill. PL20 | 26 C5 |
| Briar Tor. PL20 | 26 A5 |
| Buckland Rd. PL20 | 26 A5 |
| Clonway. PL20 | 26 A4 |
| Cox Tor Clo. PL20 | 26 A4 |
| Crapstone Rd. PL20 | 26 A5 |
| Devon Tors Rd. PL20 | 26 B5 |
| Dousland Rd. PL20 | 26 B5 |
| Eastella Rd. PL20 | 26 C5 |
| Elford Park. PL20 | 26 B5 |
| Grange Rd. PL20 | 26 A4 |
| Great Mis Tor Clo. | |
| PL20 | 26 A4 |
| Greenbank Ter. PL20 | 26 B5 |
| Grenville Pk. PL20 | 26 B5 |
| Harrowbeer La. PL20 | 26 A4 |
| Hazel Gro. PL20 | 26 B4 |
| Heathfield Pk. PL20 | 26 C4 |
| Ingra Tor. PL20 | 26 A4 |
| Kirkella Rd. PL20 | 26 C5 |
| Lake La. PL20 | 26 D4 |
| Langton Rd. PL20 | 26 B4 |
| Leather Tor Clo. PL20 | 26 B4 |
| Leg O'Mutton. PL20 | 26 A4 |
| Meavy Bourne. PL20 | 26 C5 |
| Meavy La. PL20 | 26 B5 |
| Meavy Villas. PL20 | 26 C5 |
| Midella Rd. PL20 | 26 C5 |
| Moor View Ter. PL20 | 26 B5 |
| Pew Tor Clo. PL20 | 26 B4 |
| Plymouth La. PL20 | 26 B5 |
| Plymouth Rd. PL20 | 26 B5 |
| Pound Rd. PL20 | 26 A4 |
| Princetown Rd. PL20 | 26 D4 |
| St Albans Pk. PL20 | 26 C5 |
| Southella Rd. PL20 | 26 C5 |
| Station Rd. PL20 | 26 A5 |
| Tavistock Rd. PL20 | 26 A4 |
| The Green. PL20 | 26 B5 |
| Vixen Tor Clo. PL20 | 26 B4 |
| Westella Rd. PL20 | 26 C5 |
| Willowby Pk. PL20 | 26 C5 |
| *Yelverton Ter, | |
| Meavy La. PL20 | 26 B5 |